Stained glass

First published in the UK in 2003 by
Apple Press
Sheridan House
112-116A Western Road
Hove
East Sussex BN3 1 DD
UK

ISBN 1 84092 370 9
10 9 8 7 6 5 4 3 2 1

Design: Elisabeth Gerber
Cover Image: Bobbie Bush Photography,
www.bobbiebush.com
Photographer: Bobbie Bush Photography,
www.bobbiebush.com
Copyeditor: Amy Sutton
Proofreader: Ron Hampton

Printed in China
Printed in Hong Kong
Printed in Singapore

Stained glass

Exploring New Techniques and New Materials

Giorgetta McRee
and Livia McRee

APPLE

Contents

exploring GLASS

Glass art has a timeless appeal; the mention of stained glass brings to mind antique cathedral windows and Tiffany lampshades. If glass calls to you, don't be intimidated by the seeming complexity of the craft. You'll need relatively few tools to begin, and once you've learned a few simple techniques, you'll be well on your way to discovering the rewards of this art form.

Glass work can be divided into three categories: *cold glass*, *warm glass*, and *hot glass*. In this book, we'll explore cold and warm glass techniques. Cold glass refers to working with glass at room temperature; this includes traditional soldered stained glass and surface decorating techniques such as painting and etching. Warm glass refers to fusing, slumping, and other kiln techniques; glass is heated just enough to soften and gently form it. Hot glass techniques involve a furnace, which can reach temperatures above 2000°F (1100°C); glassblowing falls into this category. Sometimes within the art glass community, "warm" and "hot" aren't differentiated, but are simply referred to as hot glass.

The projects in the cold glass section are intended to explore the many possibilities for expanding upon traditional techniques and styles. The projects in the warm glass section are intended to

introduce kiln work to the beginner. The basic techniques sections are intended to be handy reference manuals to be used again and again—each technique is described step by step, so that if you encounter a problem while you work, you can skip to the part you need with ease.

Finally, the gallery at the end of the book features gorgeous contemporary work from glass artists around the world. We hope that it inspires you to experiment, create, and learn more about glass art.

WHAT IS STAINED GLASS?

Glass is a simple, natural material. It is created when silica—sand—is melted. By mixing minerals with silica, colored or "stained" glass is made. Iron yields green glass; selenium or gold yields red; soda and lime are used to make clear glass. Once molten, the glass mixture is then rolled into a sheet by hand or machine. Using this simple procedure, artisans around the world have created glass for centuries. These days, glass is available in a dazzling variety of colors, textures, and finishes, and the best part of it is that each piece is unique.

GETTING STARTED

SETTING UP A WORK SPACE

Not every artist can have a spacious studio filled with the latest gadgets. Not to worry—there are only a few things that are crucial to stained glass work:

- An electrical outlet will be necessary for plugging in a soldering iron.
- Good lighting from several sources, such as an overhead fixture and a smaller, adjustable lamp, is extremely helpful.
- Excellent ventilation is vital—preferably from a fan installed in a window—to funnel soldering fumes away from the work area. Also, when soldering, set up an additional table fan to blow across the work-table toward the window.
- A flat, level work surface will ensure that leaded lines are even, because molten lead follows gravity.

BASIC STAINED GLASS TOOLS AND SUPPLIES

As with any well-established art, there are many specialty tools available for working with stained glass. However, there are only a few simple tools that are essential:

01. *Safety goggles* are crucial for eye protection when working with glass. Shards can fly up unexpectedly. (Not shown.)
02. *Rubber gloves* protect hands from chemicals, such as flux or patina. Heavier gloves with a rubberized gripping aid should be used when handling glass. (Not shown.)
03. *Homosote board* is made out of paper. It's available at hardware stores and building centers and comes in large sheets $1/2$" (1 cm) thick. It is commonly used in schools as bulletin boards because it holds up well when used with push pins. To prepare a homosote work surface, cut it to an appropriate size for your table. Then, make a 90-degree brace by nailing two pieces of narrow, $1/4$" (6 mm) thick wood in one of the corners. This properly squared space is helpful to hold pieces of a project tightly together.
04. *Pushpins* are very useful for holding individual pieces of foiled glass tightly together during assembly. They are also used on homosote board.
05. *Glass cutters* range from the simple ball-ended wheel cutter seen opposite to more sophisticated circle and straightedge cutters. Though they're called cutters, they actually just score glass. Tungsten-carbide wheels are best, as they produce an excellent score that requires less pressure than less expensive steel or carbide wheels. Having to press too hard for a good score will inevitably lead to a bad break.
06. *Breakers* are used to snap glass along any scored lines.
07. *Running pliers* are especially helpful when breaking along straight scored lines.
08. *Groziers* are serrated pliers that are used to grind away or "groze" the edges of cut glass to perfect the shape.

09. *Medium-grade sandpaper* for metal can be used to refine the edges of glass pieces before foiling them. Grinders are electrical machines with diamond heads that make the job easier, but aren't necessary. Other items can be used, too, such as metal files, sharpening stones, or a Dremel MiniMite fitted with a fine grinding tip. Experiment to see which tools work best for you. (Not shown.)

10. Use a *bench brush* to sweep away glass shards from the work surface on a regular basis. (Not shown.)

11. *Copper foil* is an adhesive tape that is used to wrap the edges of pieces of glass that need to be soldered.

12. Use a *burnisher* to press foil into place; the back of a spoon will do in a pinch.

13. *Flux and brushes* for applying it are needed to prepare the surface of copper foil before soldering. The foil is coated with a non metallic oxide film that often impedes solder from properly bind ing with the copper, causing it to flow unevenly when melted; applying flux prevents uneven solder flow.

14. A *soldering iron* is used to melt solder along foiled seams. Iron tips come in various sizes, and the type used depends on personal preference. Smaller $1/4$" (6 mm) tips are better for reaching smaller places and make it easier to control the flow of lead.

15. *Solder* is composed of tin and lead and is used to attach pieces of foiled glass together.

16. *Tinning blocks* are made of ammonium chloride and are used to clean and "tin" soldering iron tips. Iron tips become corroded with use, so it is necessary to wipe them off on a tinning block; this causes a chemical reaction that cleans and coats the iron tip with a thin protective coat of solder. One will last for life.

17. *Patinas* are available in many colors, such as black or verdigris, and they are used to color the soldered areas of finished works.

18. *Polish* for metal is used to protect, clean, and brighten soldered seams We highly recommend Simichrome, which is available from stained glass suppliers.

19. *Glass*, of course! Seen above are just a few of the patterns, finishes, and textures available.

THE COPPER-FOIL METHOD

Traditionally, stained glass was assembled using strips of lead called *lead came*—an awkward technique that precluded the possibility of intricate, delicate designs because of the lead came's bulk and lack of pliability. This is why many old stained glass windows have intricately painted details on large pieces of glass. In addition, only the joints can be soldered in a lead came piece. Ultrathin, flexible copper foil enables stained glass artists to create beautifully intricate pieces that are structurally sound because all the seams are completely soldered.

SAFETY! SAFETY! SAFETY!

Stained glass work involves sharp edges, chemicals, and fumes. Develop good work habits from the beginning to ensure a safe and healthy environment. Here are some basic guidelines for working with glass:

- Store glass wrapped in paper to cover sharp edges.
- Store tools and chemicals out of the reach of children and animals.
- Vacuum the work area regularly so that shards don't find their way into the rest of the house.
- Wear work gloves when handling glass as much as possible.
- Always wear safety goggles when cutting or breaking glass.
- Always use a bench brush to wipe away glass bits while cutting—never use your hands. Minor cuts will add up quickly when working with glass!
- Always wash up after handling lead and chemicals, and never eat in the work area.
- Soldering creates fumes that contain lead—without proper ventilation, these fumes can be extremely toxic. **Proper ventilation is the most important safety precaution.**

PREPARING PATTERNS

The first step in creating a stained glass work is to select a pattern. There are numerous books available with many beautiful patterns from which to choose (see Resources on page 122). There is also a pattern section in this book, starting on page 108.

Stained glass patterns need to be duplicated for each project. One will be cut apart and used as a template to create scoring guidelines on the glass. The other will be kept intact and used as reference while cutting and assembling the piece. It's also helpful to plan the color scheme of the project on a third copy, using crayons or markers.

SELECTING GLASS

The sheer variety of colors and textures of glass available today can be both exhilarating and daunting. Glass can be streaked, textured with bumps or ripples, embossed with patterns such as leaves, embedded with bubbles or crackles, or have an opalescent surface sheen. Don't be overwhelmed by all these choices—just keep a few things in mind when selecting glass:

1. When selecting glass for a particular pattern, think about where the finished piece will be displayed. What other colors will surround it? Will the light source be natural or artificial? Try to examine the glass in an area of the store that most closely approximates the display conditions.

2. If it will be displayed in a window, hold the glass up to the light to check translucency. Is the color rich enough? Glass looks completely different when stacked up in a store. That seemingly boring, solid color may glow beautifully and reveal hidden streaks when held up to the light.

3. If the finished piece will be displayed against a wall, try using opaque or opalescent glass, which retain their beauty when they're not backlit.

4. If the project is a lamp, which will be seen when lit and unlit, try to find glass that looks good both ways.

Break a straight cut using running pliers. Notice how the center mark on the pliers is aligned with the scored line.

To cut glass along a curve, remove the excess in several gently sloping pieces.

SCORING AND BREAKING ALONG A STRAIGHT LINE

Scoring and breaking glass is perhaps the most intimidating part of the process for a new stained glass artist. It requires patience, practice, and most importantly, confidence. Get a feel for the technique by practicing on scrap glass or inexpensive picture frame glass.

1. Use a straightedge, such as a metal ruler, rather than a marked line as a guide. This will ensure the cut is perfectly straight.

2. Next, put on safety goggles. Then, hold the glass cutter vertically between your index and third finger, as shown here. Position the cutter at the edge farthest from you, next to the ruler. Press down firmly on the glass, but not too firmly—about 10 pounds of pressure. Try pressing down on a scale to get a feel for this amount of pressure.

3. Continue holding the cutter vertically and slowly draw it toward you. Try to apply firm, even pressure all the while. Too much pressure will result in a grating sound and chips along the scored line. The proper amount of pressure will result in a sing-ing sound, and the scored line will look like a light scratch mark. Too little pressure, and the scored line may be hardly visible. Never go over a score line more than once. This will damage the cutter wheel and result in a bad break. Any imperfections in the cut line can be grozed off later.

4. Use the ball end of the cutter to lightly tap along the scored line.

5. To break a straight cut, use running pliers. Hold the glass steady with one hand, and align the center mark on the pliers over the scored line at the bottom edge of the glass sheet with the other hand. Then, gently squeeze the handle of the pliers.

SCORING AND BREAKING AROUND A PATTERN

1. First the glass needs to be marked. Place the template under the glass if it is fairly translucent, or use double-sided tape to adhere it to the surface if the glass is opaque or very dark. Then use a fine-tipped permanent marker to trace the template outline on the glass. Don't worry—the marks will come off when washed. Water-soluble markers tend to smear on glass. Be sure to center the pattern marking on a piece of glass that isn't too much larger than needed.

2. Put on safety goggles. Beginning at the top edge of the pattern marking, score along the edge of the pattern and off the glass once you come close to an edge, or before cutting around too much of the pattern. The excess glass will need to be removed in pieces.

3. Continue cutting around the pattern and off the edge of the glass until the whole piece is scored.

4. Using the ball end of the cutter, tap along the scored lines.

5. Working around the pattern, use a breaker to remove the excess glass. The breaker should be held perpendicular to the scored line, and placed at the end of the score line nearest you. Hold the glass steady with one hand, and hold the breaker firmly with the other; do not squeeze. Then, using both hands, separate the glass with a smooth downward motion. In the beginning, it may be more effective to break the pieces off by hand, because it is easier to feel resistant areas; tap along that area to deepen the score, and try to separate the glass again.

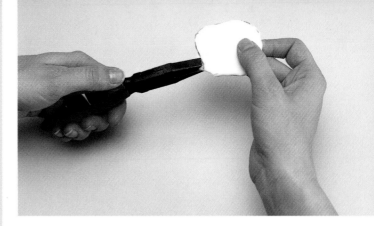

Gently chew away the excess glass using the pattern marking as a guideline.

SCORING AND BREAKING TIPS

Not every pattern is made of straight edges and gentle curves. Patterns that have fine points, circles, or semicircles take more time and patience to cut successfully. Don't be discouraged if glass breaks where it's not supposed to when cutting more complex pattern pieces—sometimes glass has inherent stress lines or fractures. In these cases, try to use the glass in a different way than planned.

Get to know glass, and in time you will be able to tell with ease what it can and can't do—and you'll even learn to predict those stress points!

- *Scoring points*: Points are a delicate area and generally won't withstand the pressure of a breaker. Always break the glass at the edge farthest from the point.
- *Scoring curves*: Inside curves in a pattern will need to be broken away in pieces to avoid a bad break. Score the glass according to the pattern as normal, but also score concentric curved lines within the inside curve, approximately 1/8" (3 mm) apart. Then, use the breaker to carefully nip the excess glass away in these 1/8" (3 mm) increments.

GROZING GLASS FOR A PERFECT FIT

Groziers are pliers with serrated jaws designed to gently chew and chip away at the edges of a cut piece of glass. The edges of cut glass shapes need to be refined to precisely fit within the project template. Therefore, grozing is a crucial step in creating a structurally sound piece of work in which all the pieces fit together perfectly.

1. Put on safety goggles. Arrange all the cut project pieces on the template.

2. Begin with one of the outer pieces. Use the tip of the grozier to remove any bumps along the edge of the glass that protrude past the template outline.

3. After the larger bumps have been removed, continue grozing until the piece matches the template as closely as possible. Don't apply too much pressure, and don't try to remove too much at once. This will cause the glass to chip.

4. Use a piece of medium-grade sandpaper suitable for metal surfaces or an electrical grinder to smooth the edges of the pieces further, so that they fit together like a puzzle.

5. Because foil is soft and easily torn, a smooth edge aids adhesion. When making three-dimensional forms such as boxes, hold adjoining sides together to make sure the edges abut perfectly. Don't overlap the edges—the outside seam should create a groove, which will eventually be filled with solder.

FOILING GLASS

Copper foil is a paper-backed, adhesive metal tape available in several sizes, from 3/16" (4.5 mm) to 1/2" (1 cm). It can have straight or decorative scalloped edges. Though all foils are copper, some are coated with brass or silver. Color choice depends on personal preference; you'll discover which you like best.

Foils also have either a silver or black backing. Because the backing color is visible after soldering in glass pieces that are translucent, silver-backed foil is good for lighter colors of glass and mirror. Blackbacked foils are good for darker glass because the color minimizes the visibility of the foil.

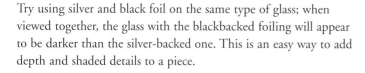

Make sure foiled edges are smooth and flat against the glass.

Notice where the pieces are tacked and how the foiled seams are still visible under the thin tinned layer.

Try using silver and black foil on the same type of glass; when viewed together, the glass with the blackbacked foiling will appear to be darker than the silver-backed one. This is an easy way to add depth and shaded details to a piece.

Also keep in mind that the width of a soldered seam depends on the size of the foil used; the wider the foil, the wider the seam. Try using different kinds of foils within the same project.

Before foiling glass, make sure the pieces are clean, dry, and free of oils or glass particles.

1. Begin foiling a glass piece about ¹/₄" (6 mm) from the end of one edge. Never begin at corners because foiled seams in these high-stress areas are likely to peel up. Center the foil on the edge of the glass and apply it slowly, pressing it to the edge and removing the paper backing as you move along.

2. Gently ease the foil around the corner, so as not to tear it. Then, crimp the foil down over the sides of the glass piece, using your fingers, from the starting point to the first corner.

3. Then, continue foiling the second edge of the glass, easing the foil around the next corner; then go back and crimp the second edge. Continue until the piece is completely foiled. Overlap the end of the foil ¹/₄" (6 mm) over the starting point.

4. Use a burnisher to press all the foiled areas along the edges and sides of the glass firmly in place.

TACKING AND TINNING

Once the glass pieces of a project are foiled, they are ready to be tacked together. This prevents the pieces from shifting during the next phase of the process, which is called *tinning*.

Tinning involves melting a thin layer of solder along all foiled areas. This strengthens the bonds between the glass pieces because the solder seeps into the crevice between pieces. Tinning also creates a base coat for beading, which results in smoother soldered lines.

1. Begin by arranging the pieces on homosote board, and use pushpins to keep them snugly together.

2. Apply flux to the foiled seams at the points where the glass pieces meet.

3. Unwind some solder from the roll, and melt off a small amount using the tip of the iron. The solder should adhere to the iron; if it doesn't, the iron isn't hot enough.

4. Touch the fluxed areas with the tip of the iron, allowing the solder to flow over the area. This serves to tack the piece together.

5. Flux all the foiled seams.

6. Melt off small amounts of solder as needed, and run the tip of the iron along the foiled seams; use just enough solder to coat them. Remember to do the back and underside of the piece.

MAKING BOXES AND THREE-DIMENSIONAL FORMS

To make boxes or other pieces with 90-degree angles, it helps to construct a right-angle holder like the one seen below, which holds the piece steady so that you have both hands free to work. It also ensures that the piece is squared during the tacking and tinning process when the seams are still flexible.

1. Always solder the seam that is parallel to the work surface because the solder will run toward it when melted.

2. Bead the interior seams of a box shape before tacking the fourth side in place. It will be much easier to maneuver inside, leaving only the last side to bead once the box is assembled.

3. To make a box or form that doesn't have 90-degree angles, use a nonmetal container stuffed with paper towels instead of a right-angle holder to hold it steady while you work. Tack two sides together, and then set them in the cradle of twisted and bunched paper towels. Use the paper towels to brace the piece at the bottom only, making sure that it is level.

When making square shapes, the foiled edges of the glass pieces abut each other to form a right angle, rather than overlapping. The crevices are then filled with solder and built up to form the seam.

BEADING

The final step in soldering a stained glass piece is to create the beads—the rounded seams between the glass pieces. The traditional method of beading is best for small, intricate areas because there's less chance of overheating the solder. The trouble with using this method for larger beads is that the solder often becomes overheated. This causes it to seep between the seams of the foiled pieces because it won't hold its shape. The solder then needs to cool off and solidify before it can be gathered up with the iron tip. Solder behaves like mercury when liquefied and runs away in small beads and drips. Giorgetta McRee developed a new technique for making straight or long beads. It's an easier method that results in smoother beads because the solder is less likely to overheat, and therefore, it doesn't need to be worked as much.

Traditional beading method for small intricate beads:
1. Touch the tip of the iron across the parallel, tinned seam.
2. At the same time, position a strip of solder next to the tip of the iron.
3. Move the iron slowly along the seam, allowing the solder to melt evenly along the foil.

McRee beading method for straight or long beads:
1. Apply flux to the tinned seam.
2. Unwind a strip of solder the length of the seam, and use the iron to "cut" it off.
3. Tack the strip in place along the seam by melting the solder strip slightly (see photograph on page 14).
4. Create the bead by running the tip of the iron along the solder strip to melt it.

To begin, this strip of solder is just barely tacked in place. Run the tip of the iron along the edges to set it, and then let it cool before continuing to smooth it out.

FINISHING TOUCHES

As with all artistic endeavors, it's often the finishing touches that pull a design together or set a piece apart from the rest. With stained glass, you'll want to treat the soldered seams because they will begin to oxidize if left alone. This oxidation results in uneven, splotchy dark spots on the silver solder. You may also want to consider framing your work, especially if it is a decorative panel that you'd like to hang rather than install. Other finishing options include:

Patina: There are several kinds of patina available. Solder can be antiqued, colored black, copper, ver-digris, brass, gray, or simply polished to retain the silver color. To apply patina, first pour it in a glass bowl and heat it on a medium setting in a microwave for ten to thirty seconds or until warm. Be careful not to overheat it. Heat facilitates the antiquing pro-cess, so additional applications won't be necessary to deepen the color. If you're working quickly and the beaded areas are still warm, heating the patina isn't necessary. Then, use a cotton swab or flux brush to slowly add patina to the seams. Build up the finish as desired. Wipe off any excess that might have seeped onto the glass; it can create a haze that's difficult to remove. Let it sit at least thirty minutes, and then rinse the piece with water.

Polishing: Use Simichrome polish to brighten and protect a patina finish. Apply several small dabs to a section of solder using a cotton swab, and then gently rub it in. Don't polish too hard or too long because the patina may start to come off.

IRON TIPS AND TEMPERATURES

Soldering irons are available in 80-watt or 100-watt voltage capability. It's best to purchase a separate temperature regulator, which can be used with any iron, rather than buying one that has a built-in regulator. These have a tendency to burn out before the iron does. Temperature plays a crucial role in manipulating solder successfully.

Generally, the larger the tip, the higher the iron temperature should be. If you want to retain detail in delicate beadwork, the iron temperature should be lower.

Once you've selected an iron, you'll want to select tips to use with it. Different tips are best suited to specific tasks (see below). Remember to clean iron tips often by wiping them on a tinning block while they are hot. Use these suggested iron settings as guidelines when beginning, and adjust as necessary:

(a) 1/8" (3 mm) flat: Set iron to 80 watts. Use for delicate or small seams.
(b) 1/4" (6 mm) flat: Set iron to 80 watts. Use for all-purpose work.
(c) 3/8" (10 mm) flat: Set iron to 100 watts. Use for wide or large seams and outside box corners.
(d) Grooved: Set iron to 80 watts. Use to create more rounded, raised beads. (Not shown.)
(e) Bent: Set iron to 80 watts. Use to make small, decorative accents or to make designs or indents in a larger bead.

Each soldering tip performs a special function.

Chapter 1

COMBINING GLASS
WITH WOOD, METAL, AND NATURAL OBJECTS

One of the most exciting ways to enhance a stained glass work is to incorporate unexpected elements. Everyone knows—or thinks they know—what to expect when they hear the words "stained glass." But this art form, though ancient and traditional, doesn't have to be predictable.

An antique silver brooch, polished gemstones, shells, and even driftwood are just a few of the things that can be successfully joined with glass. So many effects can be achieved by mixing media—both striking and subtle, and always interesting. Imagine the warm, grainy texture of wood combined with a smooth piece of swirling green glass, or a polished burgundy-colored gem surrounded by similar but lighter shades of glass.

Trial and error is one sure way to discover how best to assemble a mixed media piece—but in this chapter, you'll learn a few simple principles and techniques that will help you to create beautiful and functional art right from the start. Once you start mixing and matching, nothing's safe from the soldering iron. Be inspired to stretch the boundaries of stained glass art and make a few discoveries of your own.

Mermaid Mirror

Imagine this dreamy, mist-covered mirror adorning a bathroom wall—a perfect seashell at the top adding a delightful, unexpected accent. This shell is stained pink; some shells are polished like gemstones to reveal a gorgeous array of shimmering natural tones. Choose glass that complements colors in the shell, or use sea-inspired blues. The opalescent pink glass used here suggests the delicate sheen often found inside shells.

MATERIALS

- Basic tools and supplies (see page 8)

- $1/2$ sheet of glass (6" x 12" or 15 cm x 30 cm) pearlescent or opalescent

- Seashell

- Uncoated picture-hanging wire

- Wire cutters

DESIGNER'S TIP

Choose shells that have at least one flat side so that the mirror will hang against a wall nicely. The areas of the shell to be foiled should also be fairly uniform in thickness to ensure a secure and even bond; shells can also be minimally and gently grozed, if necessary.

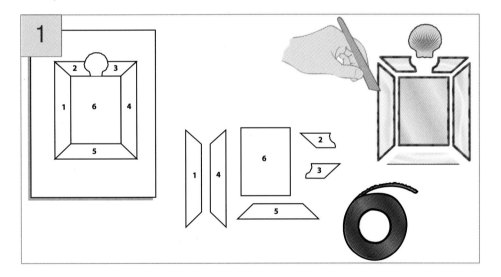

1. CUT AND FOIL THE GLASS PIECES. Prepare the pattern pieces and template (see page 109). Adjust the pattern as needed to accommodate the uniqueness of the selected shell. Score and break the glass as close as possible to the edge of the pattern pieces. Place the glass pieces on the corresponding areas of the template. Groze the edges of the glass for a snug fit, using the template as a guide. Then, foil the edges of each glass piece and the shell, making sure to center the glass edge on the foil, so that there is an even overlap on each side. Burnish the foiled areas.

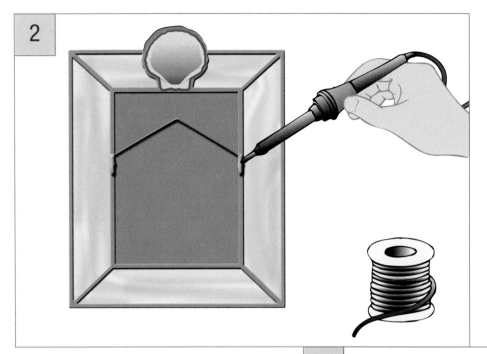

2. TACK THE SEAMS AND WIRE HANGER, THEN TIN ALL FOILED EDGES.

Arrange the foiled glass pieces on the template and use pushpins to keep them all snugly together. Brush flux on the foil at each point where the corners of the glass pieces meet. Use a small amount of solder to tack these areas together.

Add the wire hanger. Brush flux over the foiled edges. Unwind some solder from the roll. Use the tip of the iron to remove a little bit from the end of the solder strip, then run the iron over the foiled edges. Tin both the front and the back of the piece with a thin layer of solder. Be careful when turning the piece over, because the bonds will still be flexible.

Add the wire hanger. Cut a length of wire for the hanger. Brush flux on both ends of wire, covering ¹/₄" (6 mm) (or more, if making a larger or heavier mirror than the one here). Fit the wire ends into the seams on both sides of the mirror, then remove and brush flux on these tinned areas. Tack the wire in place with a small amount of solder.

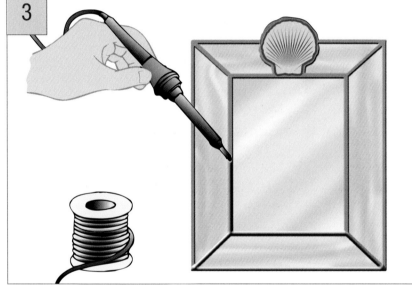

3. BEAD ALL TINNED AREAS.

Bead the piece using one of the methods described on page 14. Continue beading until all the seams are completed, and then let the piece cool completely before beading the other side. Reapply flux over tinned areas and beads in between each application of lead. If the project takes more than one day to complete, wash the piece and reapply the flux as needed.

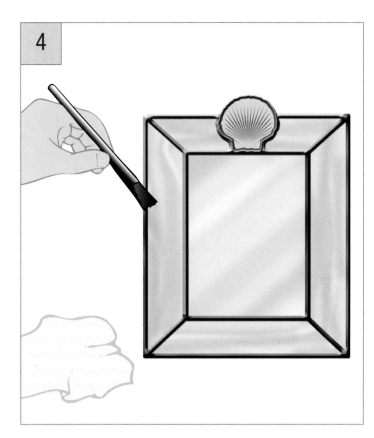

4

4. CLEAN AND FINISH THE PIECE. Once the piece has cooled, clean it with dishwashing liquid and a white sponge. Rinse well to remove all soapy residue. Dry completely with paper towels.

Apply patina of choice to the beaded areas (see page 15). Let the piece set for at least thirty minutes. Rinse with warm water and dry completely with paper towels again. Apply Simichrome polish in sparse dabs along the beaded areas, then buff gently with a soft cloth.

TRADE SECRETS

Scrap glass, which is normally destined for the trash, can be used to create a whole new work of art. It doesn't matter if they won't fit a pattern—try using them as is.

Save scraps from previous projects in clear plastic storage boxes, separated by color families. Then, lay several pieces on sturdy paper or cardboard, and play with the arrangement. Add more pieces, or take them away until something begins to take shape. This sort of project can't be predetermined; let the pieces inspire a design. Try beginning with one special piece, and then work around it.

Geode Candleholder

When geodes are first unearthed, they appear to be ordinary rocks—but once they are opened and polished, breathtaking colors and patterns are revealed. When cut thinly, like the slices used to make this candleholder, they become translucent. Test possible pieces for this project by holding them up to a candle flame; there will usually be areas of more or less translucency. Plan the positioning of the geode to accentuate the best areas.

MATERIALS

- Basic tools and supplies (see page 8)

- Right angle stand

- 1 full sheet of glass, not opaque (12" x 12" or 30 cm x 30 cm)

- Polished geode slices or other translucent gem-stones

DESIGNER'S TIP

Scrub the geode slices free of grime and sand using a toothbrush. Any particles trapped in the foil will eventually work themselves loose, even after beading.

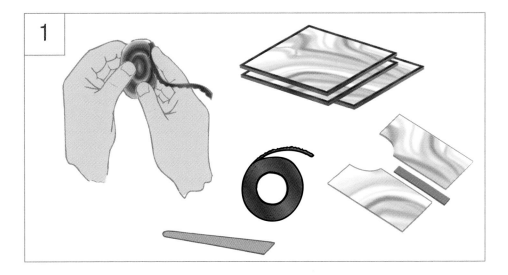

1. CUT AND FOIL THE GLASS PIECES. Prepare the pattern pieces and template (see page 110). Adjust the pattern as needed to accommodate the uniqueness of the selected geode slice. Score and break the glass as close as possible to the edge of the pattern pieces. Place the glass pieces on the corresponding areas of the template. Groze the edges of the glass for a snug fit, using the template as a guide. Then, foil the edges of each glass piece and the geode slice, making sure to center the glass edge on the foil, so that there is an even overlap on each side. Burnish the foiled areas.

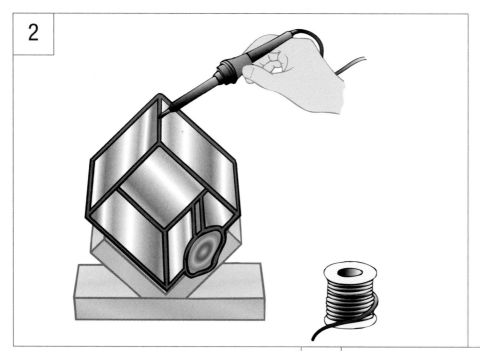

2

2. TACK THE SEAMS, THEN TIN ALL FOILED EDGES.

Assemble the sides that have multiple pieces by brushing flux on the foil at the top and the bottom where the corners of the glass pieces meet. Use a small amount of solder to tack these areas together. Then, fit two sides of the candleholder into the right-angle holder, brush with flux at the top and the bottom where the corners of the glass pieces meet, and tack together. Add a third side in the same manner. Remove from the right-angle holder. Tack the fourth side in place. Then tack the bottom in place. Return the candleholder to the right-angle holder.

Brush flux over the foiled edges. Unwind some solder from the roll. Use the tip of the iron to remove a little bit from the end of the solder strip, then run the iron over the foiled edges. Tin all sides of the piece with a thin layer of solder. Be careful when handling the piece because the bonds will still be flexible.

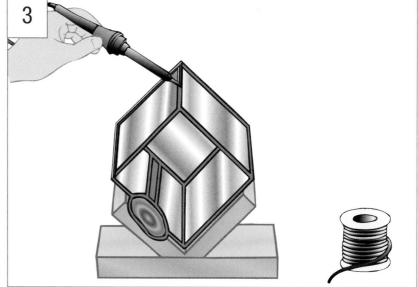

3

3. BEAD ALL TINNED AREAS.

Touch the tip of the iron across the tinned seams. At the same time, position a strip of solder next to the tip of the iron. Move the iron slowly along the seam, allowing the solder to melt evenly along the foil. Continue beading until all the seams are completed, then turn the piece over and bead the other side. Reapply flux over tinned areas and beads in between each application of lead.

Wash the piece thoroughly with a white sponge and dishwashing detergent to remove all flux. If the project takes more than one day to complete, wash the piece and reapply the flux as needed.

TRADE SECRETS

Decorative metal objects, even delicate ones such as the antique metal butterfly on the candleholder shown with the main project, can be easily incorporated into a stained glass work.

To attach metal pieces to a project, either flux the piece directly or foil the edges. Brass, silver, and copper pieces can be directly soldered after applying flux, but alloys (such as white metal) typically can't. Another alternative is to wrap or affix wire to a piece of metal, and then solder the wire. Make sure the wire is uncoated, and be sure to apply flux.

4. CLEAN AND FINISH THE PIECE. Once the piece has cooled, clean it with dishwashing liquid and a white sponge. Rinse well to remove all soapy residue. Dry completely with paper towels.

Apply patina of choice to the beaded areas. Let the piece set for at least 30 minutes. Rinse with warm water and dry completely with paper towels again. Apply Simichrome polish in sparse dabs along the beaded areas, then buff gently with a soft cloth.

Trinket Tray

This small tray is the ideal holder for small pieces of jewelry, like rings or necklaces, but the pattern could easily be enlarged to make a serving tray. The free-form carved handles, which were made especially for this piece, echo the curving patterns in the glass. Try your hand at carving a set of handles, or choose pieces of wood, such as twigs, and work with the natural shape. For a completely different look, try using dowels or store-bought drawer pulls.

MATERIALS

- Basic tools and supplies (see page 8)

- ½ sheet of glass (6" x 12" or 15 cm x 30 cm)

- Wood for handles

DESIGNER'S TIP

To securely foil wood, be sure the pieces you choose are free of rough spots, oils, and dirt. Sand if necessary, and use a damp cloth to remove the dust.

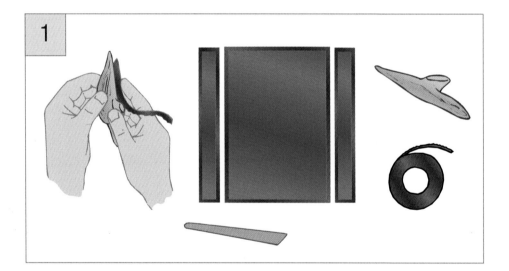

1. CUT THE GLASS AND FOIL ALL PIECES. Prepare the pattern pieces and template (see page 111). Adjust the pattern as needed to compensate for the uniqueness of the selected wood. Score and break the glass as close as possible to the edge of the pattern pieces. Place the glass pieces on the corresponding areas of the template. Groze the edges of the glass for a snug fit, using the template as a guide. Then, foil the edges of each glass piece and the wood, making sure to center the glass edge on the foil, so that there is an even overlap on each side. Use wide foil for the wood pieces to ensure that the soldered seam will be big enough to handle the stress of use. Burnish the foiled areas.

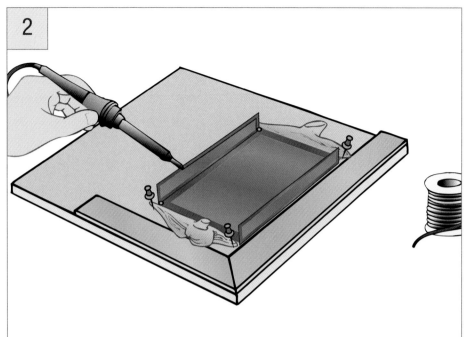

2. TACK THE SEAMS, AND THEN TIN ALL FOILED EDGES.
Position the bottom and sides of the tray against the
table brace, and use pushpins to hold everything
together. Brush flux on the foil at each point where
the corners of the glass pieces meet. Use a small
amount of solder to tack these areas together.

Brush flux over the foiled edges. Unwind some solder
from the roll. Use the tip of the iron to remove a little
bit from the end of the solder strip, and then run the
iron over the foiled edges. Tin all seams with a thin
layer of solder. Be careful when handling the piece
because the bonds will still be flexible. Once cool,
turn the piece over and tin the bottom.

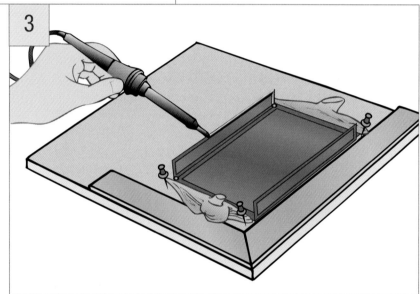

3. BEAD ALL TINNED AREAS. Bead the piece using one of the methods
described on page 15. Continue beading until all the seams are
completed, and then let the piece cool completely before beading
the other side. Reapply flux over tinned areas and beads in between
each application of lead. If the project takes more than one day to
complete, wash the piece and reapply the flux as needed.

4. CLEAN AND FINISH THE PIECE. Once the piece has cooled, clean it with dishwashing liquid and a white sponge. Rinse well to remove all soapy residue. Dry completely with paper towels.

Apply patina of choice to the beaded areas (see page 15). Let the piece set for at least thirty minutes. Rinse with warm water and dry completely with paper towels again. Apply Simichrome polish in sparse dabs along the beaded areas, and then buff gently with a soft cloth.

TRADE SECRETS

Wood is easily scorched by the heat of soldering irons, so use caution when assembling your project. Keep in mind that harder woods such as oak or maple won't scorch as easily as pine and other soft woods. Of course, softer woods can be used with care, and wood-burned accents could add to a rustic look.

Experiment with incorporating store-bought wood trims or appliqués with glass; the usually traditional designs of such items will lend a classic appeal to a project. A lacy, open appliqué could be used to make the perfect focal point for the top of an old-fashioned potpourri container.

Chapter 2

DECORATIVE
SURFACE TECHNIQUES

The beauty of glass can be further enhanced with surface decorating techniques such as painting, etching, and engraving. These techniques allow the artist to truly personalize a piece; the potential for self-statement increases exponentially with the addition of these simple skills to your repertoire.

Painted details can be kiln fired, oven baked, or air dried, giving the modern glass artist a variety of colors and effects from which to choose. Etching, in contrast, works by removing the surface layer of glass, producing a matte effect. It is an intriguing and often subtle way to enhance your work. Etched designs are created using stencils, which you can purchase or design yourself using adhesive vinyl. Experiment with the interplay between etched and unetched surfaces, which will affect the way a piece diffuses light dramatically. Engraving tools produce a similar matte effect; they allow you to draw designs on glass, which is particularly appealing. These tools aren't simply for signing your name!

More advanced techniques for surface decoration include sandblasting and kiln-fired painting. You'll see some beautiful examples of these techniques in the Gallery of Art Glass, which begins on page 86.

Tulip Vase

The tulip on this elegant, functional vase was cut so that the streaks in the glass are positioned vertically, which is reminiscent of how real petals would unfold. The addition of a painted highlight at the top completes the effect of a blossoming tulip. Simple but effective, the painted accents were created using glass stains specially formulated for stained glass work. The stains hold up to handling and washing and will remain glossy without being heat set.

MATERIALS

- Basic tools and supplies (see page 8)

- 1 full sheet of pale yellow glass (12" x 12" or 30 cm x 30 cm)

- Scrap of glass for tulip, medium yellow

- Color Magic glass stains (see Resources, page 122)

- Paintbrush

DESIGNER'S TIP

This vase has small feet, which are made by melting a little extra solder and allowing it to pool at each corner seam. Practice this technique on scraps first, making sure that the seam is perpendicular to a level work surface.

1. CUT AND FOIL THE GLASS PIECES. Prepare the pattern pieces and template (see page 112). Score and break the glass as close as possible to the edge of the pattern pieces. Place the glass pieces on the corresponding areas of the template. Groze the edges of the glass for a snug fit, using the template as a guide. Then, foil the edges of each glass, making sure to center the glass edge on the foil, so that there is an even overlap on each side. Burnish the foiled areas. The top edges of this vase were left unfoiled. See Trade Secrets on page 35.

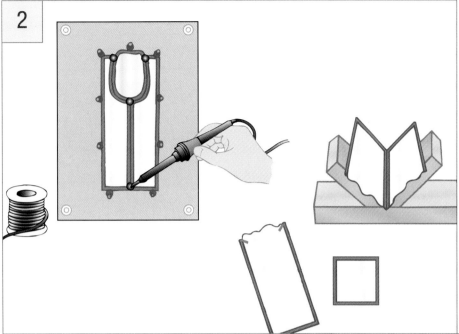

2. TACK THE SEAMS, AND THEN TIN ALL FOILED EDGES.
Arrange the foiled glass pieces of the front of the vase
on the template and use pushpins to keep them all
snugly together. Brush flux on the foil at each point
where the corners of the glass pieces meet. Use a small
amount of solder to tack these areas together.

Then, fit two adjoining sides of the vase into the right
angle holder. Brush flux on the foil at the top and the
bottom where the corners of the glass pieces meet. Use
a small amount of solder to tack these areas together.
Add a third side in the same manner. Remove from
the right-angle holder. Tack the fourth side in place.
Then tack the bottom in place. Return the vase to the
right-angle holder.

Brush flux over the foiled edges. Unwind some solder from the
roll. Use the tip of the iron to remove a little bit from the end of
the solder strip, and then run the iron over the foiled edges. Tin
both the inside and outside of the piece with a thin layer of solder. Be careful when handling the piece because the bonds will
still be flexible.

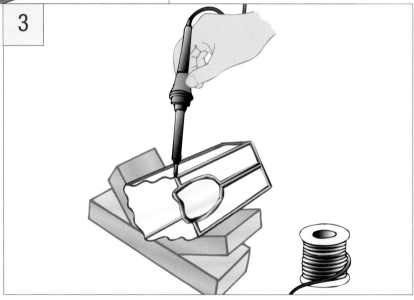

3. BEAD ALL TINNED AREAS. Place the vase in the right-angle holder
with a seam parallel to the work surface. Bead the piece using one
of the methods described on page 14. Continue beading until all
the seams are completed, and then place the piece on the work surface and bead the top and inside bottom seams, which will be parallel to the work surface. Reapply flux over tinned areas and beads
in between each application of lead. If the project takes more than
one day to complete, wash the piece and reapply the flux as needed.

Once the piece has cooled, clean it with dishwashing liquid and a
white sponge. Rinse well to remove all soapy residue. Dry completely with paper towels.

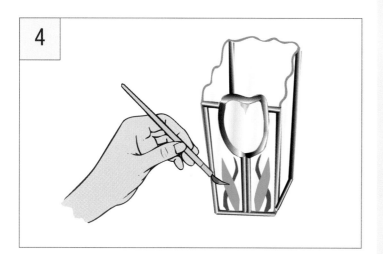

4. PAINT ACCENTS AND FINISH THE PIECE. Apply patina of choice to the beaded areas (see page 15). Let the piece set for at least thirty minutes. Rinse with warm water and dry completely with paper towels again. Apply Simichrome polish in sparse dabs along the beaded areas, and then buff gently with a soft cloth.

Paint the leaves and the tulip highlight. Practice painting on pieces of scrap glass first to get a feel for how the stains work. As with most glass paints, stains have a limited workability time, so practice brush strokes and try to minimize the amount needed to achieve the desired effect. It's also helpful to experiment with brushes of different sizes and shapes. Color Magic glass stains can also be used on solder; the tulip stem here was painted with green stain that was then wiped off, creating a subtle wash of color.

TRADE SECRETS

The top edges of the sides and back of this vase are not foiled. Rather, the natural free-form edge of the glass sheet is used as is. This adds an additional element of interest and works wonderfully in a piece with a nature-inspired theme. Choose a glass sheet that doesn't have chips or sharp areas on the edge.

Try this easy technique for an attractive bead when partially foiling a piece: Leave tails of extra foil approximately 1/4" (6 mm) past the edge of the seams adjacent to the unfoiled areas. Tin the excess along with the rest of the seams. When beading the seams, allow the bead to extend to this tail, but don't worry about making it look good. Then, trim the excess neatly with a craft knife and burnish the edge.

The natural edge of a glass sheet inspired this compostition.

Art Deco Napkin Holder

The geometric shape combined with the silver and black color scheme of this napkin holder is reminiscent of Art Deco designs, which is an artistic style that began in the 1920s. Dragonflies were also a popular motif used by Art Deco artisans. The unbroken surface of this piece is the perfect place to add an etched detail, like the dragonfly seen here. Consult art history or clip art books for other decorative motifs in this style.

MATERIALS

- Basic tools and supplies (see page 8)

- ½ sheet of black glass (6" x 12" or 15 cm x 30 cm)

- Scrap of white glass for base

- Clear adhesive vinyl

- Etchall glass etching creme

- Etchall squeegee applicator

- Etchall swivel knife

- Rubber gloves

DESIGNER'S TIP

Scalloped copper foil was used on the bottom edge of this piece. When foiling edges that will be joined with another piece of glass at a 90-degree angle, be sure that at least 1/8" (3 mm) of foil covers the inside edges to ensure a sturdy seam.

1. CUT, ETCH, AND FOIL THE GLASS PIECES. Prepare the pattern pieces and template (see page 113). Score and break the glass as close as possible to the edge of the pattern pieces. Place the glass pieces on the corresponding areas of the template.

Photocopy the etching pattern on page 113. Cut out the black areas to make a stencil; trace this outline on a piece of adhesive vinyl using a permanent marker. Use a swivel craft knife to carefully cut the pattern out of the vinyl. Firmly press the vinyl pattern to the glass. Following the manufacturer's directions, apply a thick, even layer of creme to the glass with a squeegee applicator. Wait five minutes, and then use the applicator to scrape off as much of the creme as possible and put it back in the bottle. Rinse off the remaining creme under warm running water, and remove the vinyl pattern. Be sure to wear rubber gloves when working with etching creme.

Groze the edges of the glass for a snug fit, using the template as a guide. Then, foil the edges of each glass piece, making sure to center the glass edge on the foil, so that there is an even overlap on each side. Burnish the foiled areas.

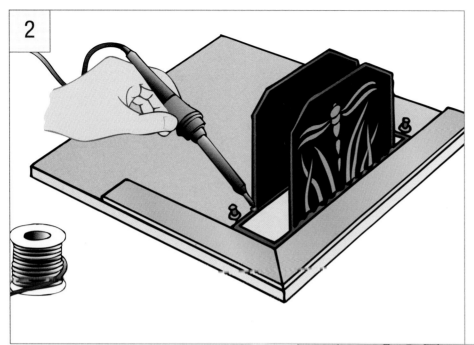

2. TACK THE SEAMS, AND THEN TIN ALL FOILED EDGES.

Position one side of the napkin holder against the right edge of the table brace. Position the bottom of the holder so that it is against and centered along this side of the napkin holder. Slide the pieces into the corner, so that the short edge of the bottom piece is snug against the bottom brace. Position the other side and use pushpins to hold everything in place. Brush flux on the foil at each point where the corners of the glass pieces meet. Use a small amount of solder to tack these areas together.

Brush flux over the foiled edges. Unwind some solder from the roll. Use the tip of the iron to remove a little bit from the end of the solder strip, and then run the iron over the foiled edges. Tin all seams with a thin layer of solder. Be careful when handling the piece because the bonds will still be flexible. Once the piece is cool, turn it over and tin the bottom.

3. BEAD ALL TINNED AREAS. Bead the piece using one of the methods described on page 14. Continue beading until all the seams are completed, and then let the piece cool completely before beading the other side. Reapply flux over tinned areas and beads in between each application of lead. If the project takes more than one day to complete, wash the piece and reapply the flux as needed.

4. CLEAN AND FINISH THE PIECE. Once the piece has cooled, clean it with dishwashing liquid and a white sponge. Rinse well to remove all soapy residue. Dry completely with paper towels.

Apply patina of choice to the beaded areas (see page 15). Let the piece set for at least thirty minutes. Rinse with warm water and dry completely with paper towels again. Apply Simichrome polish in sparse dabs along the beaded areas, and then buff gently with a soft cloth.

TRADE SECRETS

Glass etching is a wonderful way to add surface designs to stained glass—the interplay between matte and shiny surfaces can be bold or subtle, depending on the glass chosen. Etching on black glass creates the most contrast—the result indeed looks frosted.

When planning an etched design, test the etching creme on the selected glass. In general, the darker the glass, the more visible the etching will be, but also consider where the item will be displayed. If the piece will be blasted by natural light, the etching will probably be barely noticeable. An indoor setting with mostly indirect but bright light will usually show off the design best.

Sandblasting produces an effect similar to etching, but results in a reverse-relief. The white-on-white design creates an ethereal look.

Mooncatcher

You've seen suncatchers in gift stores that abound in sunny locales. Why not make a mooncatcher like the one seen here? An etched design on deep blue glass creates a mysterious, moody look befitting the moon. Finely engraved details add more depth to the etched area, giving this moon character. Try cutting a crescent-shaped piece of glass, or assembling small stars. Hang them all together in a window for a lovely mobile effect.

MATERIALS

- Basic stained glass tools and supplies (see page 15)

- ¹/₂ sheet of cobalt glass, 6" x 12" (15 cm x 30 cm)

- Adhesive vinyl

- Etchall glass etching creme

- Etchall squeegee applicator

- Etchall swivel knife

- Rubber gloves

- Engraving tool

- 20-gauge copper wire

- Wire cutters

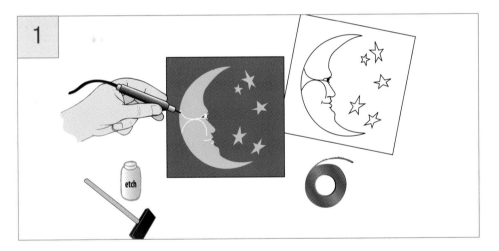

1. CUT, ETCH, AND FOIL THE GLASS PIECE. Prepare the pattern piece and template (see page 114). Score and break the glass as closely as possible to the edge of the pattern piece. Place the glass piece on the corresponding area of the template.

Photocopy the etching pattern on page 114. Cut out the black areas to make a stencil; trace this outline on a piece of adhesive vinyl using a permanent marker. Use a swivel craft knife to carefully cut the pattern out of the vinyl. Firmly press the vinyl pattern to the glass. Following the manufacturer's directions, use the creme to etch the glass. Be sure to wear rubber gloves when working with etching creme. Accentuate the facial features in the design as desired using an engraving tool. See Trade Secrets, page 43. Groze the edges of the glass for a snug fit, using the template as a guide. Then, foil the edges of each glass piece, making sure to center the glass edge on the foil, so that there is an even overlap on each side. Burnish the foiled areas.

DESIGNER'S TIP

Try using permanent marker over engraved lines to highlight certain areas. The mouth and eye on the piece seen here were highlighted using a black marker.

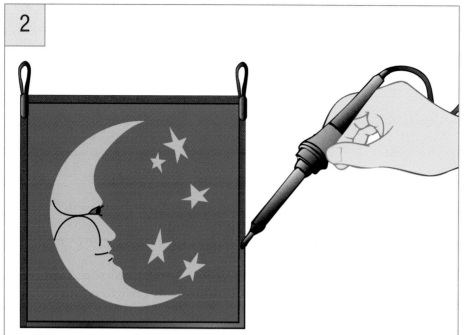

**2. TACK THE HANGERS IN PLACE AND TIN ALL FOILED
EDGES.** Twist the copper wire into loops to create the
hangers. Brush flux on the loops and the topside edges
of the mooncatcher. Use a small amount of solder to
tack the loops in place.

Brush flux over the foiled edges. Unwind some solder
from the roll. Use the tip of the iron to remove a little
bit from the end of the solder strip, and then run the
iron over the foiled edges. Tin all seams with a thin
layer of solder. Once cool, turn the piece over and tin
the back.

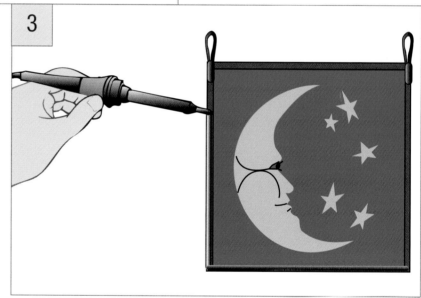

3. BEAD ALL TINNED AREAS. Bead the piece using one of the methods
described on page 14. Continue beading until all the seams are
completed, and then let the piece cool completely before beading
the other side. Reapply flux over tinned areas and beads in between
each application of lead. If the project takes more than one day to
complete, wash the piece and reapply the flux as needed.

4. CLEAN AND FINISH THE PIECE. Once the piece has cooled, clean it with dishwashing liquid and a white sponge. Rinse well to remove all soapy residue. Dry completely with paper towels.

Apply patina of choice to the beaded areas (see page 15). Let the piece set for at least thirty minutes. Rinse with warm water and dry completely with paper towels again. Apply Simichrome polish in sparse dabs along the beaded areas, and then buff gently with a soft cloth.

TRADE SECRETS

Engraving tools are inexpensive and very simple to use. The diamond-coated tip lightly carves glass, leaving a white line on any color of glass.

Hold the tool as you would a pencil or paintbrush. You can control the thickness of the lines by applying more or less pressure. For a very fine line, just barely graze the surface of the glass. Try to maintain the amount of pressure to create a line of consistent thickness. Don't draw over the same line too many times, as this will cause the glass to chip.

Chapter 3

CREATIVE
FOILING AND BEADWORK

Often overlooked are the humble foil and solder that keep stained glass works together, but just because these seams are necessary doesn't mean they have to look utilitarian. In fact, soldering can be the focal point of a piece and is always a crucial part of any overall design. After you've learned how to construct a simple, elegant bead, it's time to explore.

One easy way to spice up your soldered lines is to use scalloped foil. Foil also comes in different sizes; take advantage of this by creating seams of various widths in the same piece. Thicker lines will accentuate an area, attracting the viewer's eye. Or, skip the seams altogether, and try decoratively cutting foil and adhering it to the surface of glass, as in the Tree Tea Light project on page 54.

Even if your foiled seams are straightforward, you can add texture to your beadwork by sculpting solder. See Iron Tips and Temperatures on page 15 for advice on how to manipulate solder effectively, and you'll be well on your way to on creating striking dimensional beads.

Cabochon Jewelry Box

The leopard skin jasper cabochon that adorns this box is characterized by swirls and dots of beautiful, earthy colors. The voluptuous beadwork that surrounds it was inspired by the patterns inherent in the stone. Design a box like this one by first selecting a stone. Bring the stone along when selecting glass, and choose pieces that match the more subtle colors in the rock. This will visually draw out and enhance the natural patterns.

MATERIALS

- Basic stained glass tools and supplies (see page 8)

- Right-angle holder

- 1 full sheet of glass or different pieces to equal 1 full sheet, 12" x 12" (30 cm x 30 cm)

- Polished gemstone cabochon, washed and dried

- Jewelry chain

- Brass tube and wire set for box making (see Resources, page 122)

- Brass ball feet (optional)

- Hobby saw

- Wire cutters

DESIGNER'S TIP

Add ball feet to a box to give it a special touch. Simply apply flux to the feet and the bottom of the box where they will be attached, and then tack and solder in place.

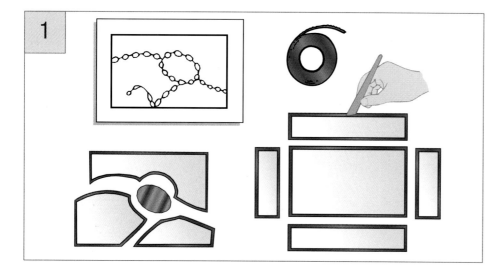

1. CUT AND FOIL THE GLASS PIECES. Prepare the pattern pieces and template (see page 115). Adjust the pattern as needed to compensate for the uniqueness of the selected gemstone cabochon. Score and break the glass as closely as possible to the edge of the pattern pieces. Place the glass pieces on the corresponding areas of the template. Groze the edges of the glass for a snug fit, using the template as a guide. Then, foil the edges of each glass piece and the cabochon, making sure to center the glass edge on the foil, so that there is an even overlap on each side. Burnish the foiled areas.

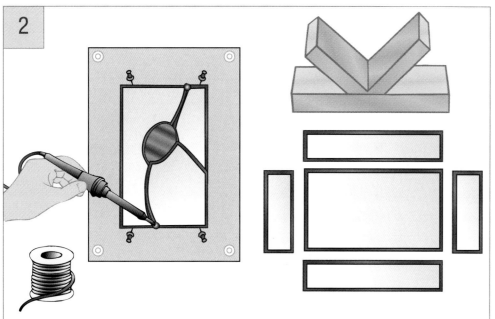

2. TACK THE SEAMS, AND THEN TIN ALL FOILED EDGES.

Arrange the foiled glass pieces of box top on the template and use pushpins to keep them all snugly together. Brush flux on the foil at each point where the corners of the glass pieces meet. Use a small amount of solder to tack these areas together. Set the top aside.

Then, fit two adjoining sides of the box base into the right-angle holder. Brush flux on the foil at the top and the bottom where the corners of the glass pieces meet. Use a small amount of solder to tack these areas together. Add a third side in the same manner. Remove from the right-angle holder. Tack the fourth side in place. Then tack the bottom in place. Return the box to the right-angle holder.

Brush flux over the foiled edges. Unwind some solder from the roll. Use the tip of the iron to remove a little bit from the end of the solder strip, and then run the iron over the foiled edges. Tin both the inside and outside of the box base and the separate box top with a thin layer of solder. Be careful when handling the box because the bonds will still be flexible.

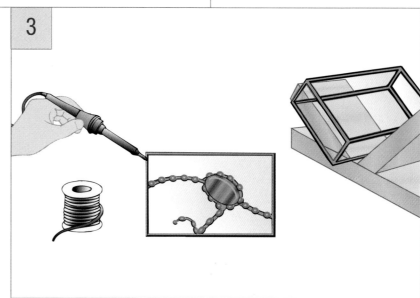

3. BEAD ALL TINNED AREAS. Place the box base in the right-angle holder with a seam parallel to the work surface. Bead the piece using one of the methods described on page 14. Continue beading until all the seams are completed, but leave the two back inside corner seams simply tinned; this is where the box top attachments will be made. Then, place the piece on the work surface and bead the other three top seams, which will be parallel to the work surface. Also bead the box top, leaving the back edge simply tinned.

Reapply flux over tinned areas and beads in between each application of lead. If the project takes more than one day to complete, wash the piece and reapply the flux as needed.

Once the piece has cooled, clean it with dishwashing liquid and a white sponge. Rinse well to remove all soapy residue. Dry completely with paper towels.

The beadwork on this box has much more dimension than a standard semicircular bead. The secret to successful dimensional beadwork is to melt off small pieces of solder, position them on seams, and then dab the edges to secure. Try to minimize melting, rather completely melting the solder as in the traditional method.

When working on a long seam, work in small sections. Let beads cool enough so that they haze over, about a minute or so, and then continue along the seam. This will lessen the chance of accidentally melting the previous bead.

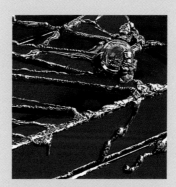

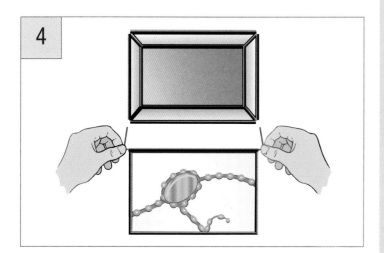

4. ATTACH THE BOX TOP AND FINISH THE PIECE. Using a hobby saw, trim the brass tube $^1/_4$" (6 mm) to $^1/_2$" (1 cm) shorter than the back edge of box top. Center the tube along the back edge of the box top and use pushpins to secure both to the work surface. Brush flux on the tube and the edge of the box top, and then tack, tin, and bead the seam. Next, cut a piece of the brass wire and thread it through the tube, so that it extends out of the tube about 1" (2.5 cm) at both ends. Place the box top on the box base. Bend the 1" (2.5 cm) wire ends outside the box, nestling them in the outside corner seams. Tack, tin, and then bead over the wires.

Use wire cutters to trim a piece of jewelry chain obviously longer than needed. Flux 1" (2.5 cm) of the chain end and a beaded seam close to one side on the box top, about 1" (2.5 cm) down from what will be the front (opening) edge. Tack and solder the chain in place. Hold the top open as much as you want, and then trim the chain leaving $^1/_2$" (1 cm) extra. Nestle the chain inside the corner of the box directly below where the chain is attached to the box top. Tack and solder the chain in place.

Apply patina of choice to the beaded areas (see page 15). Let the piece set for at least thirty minutes. Rinse with warm water and dry completely with paper towels again. Apply Simichrome polish in sparse dabs along the beaded areas, and then buff gently with a soft cloth.

Bird in Flight

This panel incorporates both straight and scalloped foil. Combining these shapes is an easy way to incorporate interesting beadwork into a piece. When planning a design, carefully consider where to place the seams. The ruffled bead near the shell here suggests downy feathers, but when the rippled edges extend into the space around the bird, they suggest movement, air currents, and clouds. The straight beads continue the line of the beak and tail gracefully, adding to the fluidity of the design.

MATERIALS

- Basic stained glass tools and supplies (see page 8)

- 1 full sheet of glass or different pieces to equal 1 full sheet, 12" x 12" (30 cm x 30 cm)

- Seashell

- Sturdy chain for hanging

- Copper channel framing (optional)

- Craft knife

- Wire cutters

DESIGNER'S TIP

To frame a piece with the copper channel seen here, cut a strip about 2" (5 cm) longer than needed to encompass the panel. Wrap the channel around the panel, notching the corners with a craft knife so they overlap neatly. Trim the excess, and then flux and solder the ends at one corner.

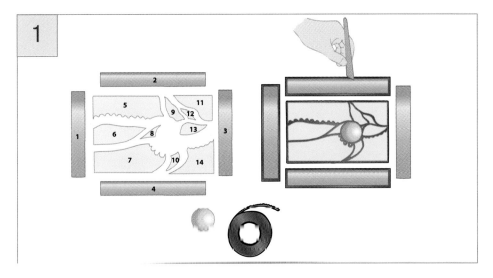

1. CUT AND FOIL THE GLASS PIECES. Prepare the pattern pieces and template (see page 116). Adjust the pattern as needed to compensate for the uniqueness of the selected shell. Score and break the glass as closely as possible to the edge of the pattern pieces. Place the glass pieces on the corresponding areas of the template. Groze the edges of the glass for a snug fit, using the template as a guide. Then foil the edges of each glass piece and the shell, making sure to center the glass edge on the foil, so that there is an even overlap on each side. Burnish the foiled areas.

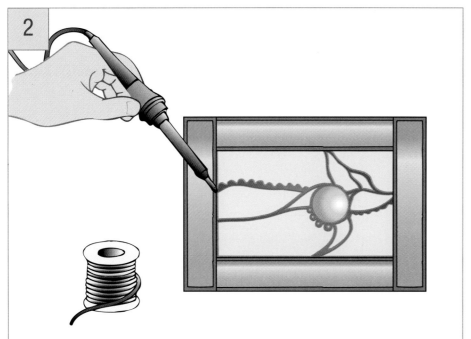

2. TACK THE SEAMS, AND THEN TIN ALL FOILED EDGES.

Arrange the foiled glass pieces on the template and use pushpins to keep them snugly together. Brush flux on the foil at each point where the corners of the glass pieces meet. Use a small amount of solder to tack these areas together.

Brush flux over the foiled edges. Unwind some solder from the roll. Use the tip of the iron to remove a little bit from the end of the solder strip, and then run the iron over the foiled edges. Tin both the front and the back of the piece with a thin layer of solder. Be careful when turning the piece over because the bonds will still be flexible.

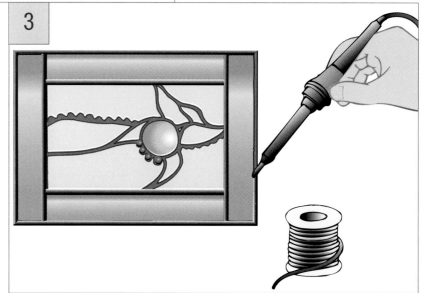

3. BEAD ALL TINNED AREAS.
Bead the piece using one of the methods described on page 14. Continue beading until all the seams are completed, and then let the piece cool completely before beading the other side. Reapply flux over tinned areas and beads in between each application of lead. If the project takes more than one day to complete, wash the piece and reapply the flux as needed.

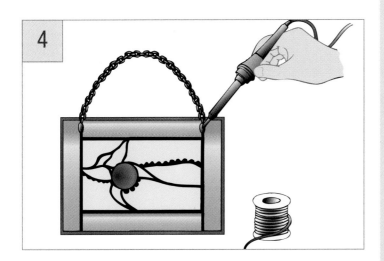

4. CLEAN AND FINISH THE PIECE. Once the piece has cooled, clean it with dishwashing liquid and a white sponge. Rinse well to remove all soapy residue. Dry completely with paper towels.

Apply patina of choice to the beaded areas (see page 15). Let the piece set for at least thirty minutes. Rinse with warm water and dry completely with paper towels again. Apply Simichrome polish in sparse dabs along the beaded areas, and then buff gently with a soft cloth.

Attach the chain for hanging by cutting a length of chain. Flux 1" (2.5 cm) of the chain ends and the vertical beaded seams on the left and right sides of the panel, beginning just under the copper channel, if framing the piece (see Designer's Tip). Tack and solder the chain in place.

TRADE SECRETS

Beaded accents can be built up by adding successive layers of solder. To do this, it's imperative to let each layer of solder cool completely to the touch. Add the next layer quickly, and let it cool again. If you make a mistake, wait until the layer has cooled to fix it. Applying heat for too long will melt all previous layers.

To create a rippled or "combed" bead, set the soldering iron to a low or medium setting. Then, gently push ripples into a rounded bead. The lower temperature allows more time to shape the solder without melting it completely.

Tree Tea Light

This elegant tree design is created entirely of foil and solder. When a solid design such as this one is layered on translucent glass, light is cast around the image so that it seems to glow, creating a romantic, ethereal mood. To create the dimensional look of this tree, first build up layers of solder, and then use a cool iron to give the tree barklike details. See Iron Tips and Temperature on page 15, and Trade Secrets on page 57 for information on sculpting solder.

MATERIALS

- Basic stained glass tools and supplies (see page 8)

- ½ sheet of translucent glass, 6" x 12" (15 cm x 30 cm)

- 3 scraps of glass for the base

DESIGNER'S TIP

Try using a heavily textured glass, which diffuses light in interesting and often unusual ways, to make candleholders. The glass used here has deep linear ridges on the back.

1. CUT AND FOIL THE GLASS PIECES. Prepare the pattern pieces and template (see page 117). Score and break the glass as closely as possible to the edge of the pattern pieces. Place the glass pieces on the corresponding areas of the template.

Groze the edges of the glass for a snug fit, using the template as a guide. Then, foil the edges of each glass piece, making sure to center the glass edge on the foil so that there is an even overlap on each side. Burnish the foiled areas. Create the tree design by burnishing foil on the front piece of the holder (see Trade Secrets, page 57).

2. TACK THE SEAMS, AND THEN TIN ALL FOILED EDGES.

Position the pieces for the base of the holder against
the table brace and use pushpins to hold everything in
place. Brush flux on the foil at each point where the
corners of the glass pieces meet. Use a small amount
of solder to tack these areas together. Align the front
of the holder against the table brace. Position the base
and the back piece against the front piece and use
pushpins to hold everything in place. Flux and tack
the piece together.

Brush flux over the foiled edges. Unwind some solder
from the roll. Use the tip of the iron to remove a little
bit from the end of the solder strip, and then run the
iron over the foiled edges. Tin all seams with a thin
layer of solder. Be careful when handling the piece
because the bonds will still be flexible. Once the
piece is cool, turnit over and tin the bottom.

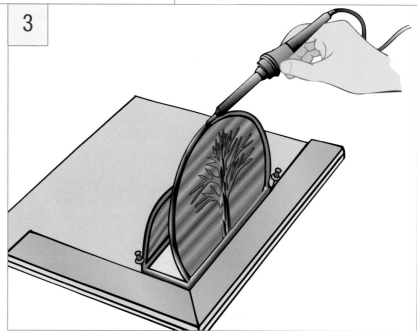

3. BEAD ALL TINNED AREAS. Bead the piece using one of the methods described on page 14. Continue beading until all the seams are
completed, and then let the piece cool completely before beading
the other side. Build up layers of solder to create a dimensional
look, if desired. Reapply flux over tinned areas and beads in between each application of lead. If the project takes more than one
day to complete, wash the piece and reapply the flux as needed.

4. CLEAN AND FINISH THE PIECE. Once the piece has cooled, clean it with dishwashing liquid and a white sponge. Rinse well to remove all soapy residue. Dry completely with paper towels.

Apply patina of choice to the beaded areas (see page 15). Let the piece set for at least thirty minutes. Rinse with warm water and dry completely with paper towels again. Apply Simichrome polish in sparse dabs along the beaded areas, and then buff gently with a soft cloth.

TRADE SECRETS

To create a superficial soldered design, split and shape wide foil with a craft knife as you adhere it to the surface of the glass. The pieces should be 1" (2.5 cm) or longer to ensure durability. Also experiment with scalloped foil and different widths. To prevent the design from peeling away from the glass, be sure to secure the ends of the foil around the bottom or side edges of the glass.

It's easy to create your own unique designs; simply sketch or trace a line drawing of the desired image. Then, slip the drawing under the glass to use as a guideline.

GETTING STARTED

There are only a few supplies you'll need to get started; they are described in the following list.

When setting up your work space, the most important consideration is the kiln. Be sure to keep it out of the reach of children, pets, and flammable material; make sure there is adequate ventilation; and make sure the electrical outlet is equipped to conduct the amount of energy required by the kiln. Read the owner's manual thoroughly, as this contains all the specific information you'll need to ensure safety.

BASIC FUSED GLASS TOOLS AND SUPPLIES

01. A *fusing glass kiln* is the most expensive and important piece of equipment needed for warm glass techniques. Though ceramic kilns can be used, it's best to purchase a kiln designed for fusing. Kilns are carefully calibrated instruments, and you'll get the best results from a kiln designed to suit your purpose.

02. *Kiln wash and kiln paper* are used to protect the interior surfaces of the kiln from the fusing glass. Without this separating layer, glass would stick to the kiln. Kiln wash is applied wet and allowed to dry; kiln paper is therefore faster and easier. Be sure that the paper is intended for glass fusing kilns, so it won't burn.

03. *Kiln shelves and molds* are used to support glass during fusing and slumping. These accessories can be purchased from glass fusing and kiln suppliers. Stainless steel objects, such as mixing bowls, also make ideal molds for slumping.

04. The same *glass cutting tools and groziers* used for cold glass techniques can be used to cut and shape glass prior to fusing. See Basic Stained Glass Tools and Supplies on page 8.

05. *Safety equipment* such as rubber gloves and particle masks. Wear gloves when handling kiln paper, and wear a particle mask when mixing kiln wash. Of course, when cutting glass, be sure to where safety goggles (see Safety! Safety! Safety! on page 10).

Photo courtesy of Skutt Kilns.

SELECTING GLASS

Any glass can be used for warm glass techniques, however, glass specially formulated for fusing and slumping is much easier to work with because it is designed to give consistent, satisfactory results.

GLASS COMPATIBILITY

The beauty of fused pieces is usually due to unique and interesting combinations of glass. When planning glass combinations, you'll need to know whether the glass is compatible.

When glass is heated and cooled during the fusing process, it expands and contracts at a specific rate. If you use two pieces of glass with different expansion and contraction rates, the piece may crack—or worse, shatter—when the piece cools. This characteristic is referred to as the coefficient of expansion (COE).

Don't worry—you don't need to be a scientist to fuse glass. Manufacturers who sell glass for fusing test for compatibility, and list the COE of their product. For example, Spectrum System 96™ glass, made by Uroboros Glass, has a COE of 96. All of the glass in this product line is compatible with each other, making glass selection easy (see Resources on page 122).

TALKING GLASS

There are many kinds of glass to choose from; new glass formulas are always being developed. In addition, some types of glass have decorative coatings, which expands the palette even further. Below is a list of terms that are used to describe specific attributes of glass.

- **Cathedral** glass is simply translucent colored glass. Opaque glass is often referred to as opalescent glass.
- **Stained glass** used for cold techniques can also be used for fusing and is sometimes referred to as art glass.
- **Iridescent glass** is any glass that has been treated with an iridescent coating, which is only superficial. Keep in mind that when the piece is lit from behind, the iridescence won't be visible. Some coatings will burn off in the kiln, unless the glass is specially formulated for fusing.
- **Dichroic glass** is coated with a film that creates a special optical effect: The glass appears to be different colors when viewed at different angles. It is available in a range of color combinations, textures, and patterns.

BEYOND FLAT SHEET GLASS

Add texture to a project by experimenting with the various shapes and sizes of glass available from suppliers for warm glass techniques.

- *Rods* are round cylinders of glass that are available in various thicknesses. Try cutting them into slices to create "millefiore" designs.
- *Stringers* are thin threads of glass that can be softened and manipulated using the heat from a candle. Try weaving them to create a fabric texture.
- *Confetti* (also called shards) is very thin slices of glass that can be layered over other colors to paint designs.
- *Frit* refers to small, irregularly shaped glass pieces, ranging from powder to chunks. Sprinkle some over a project to add a colorful pattern.

TESTING GLASS COMPATIBILITY

Once you become comfortable with the fusing process, you will probably be itching to try glass beyond that sold for fusing. Try this simple test to discover how the glass you've chosen will hold up under pressure:

1. Fuse small pieces of the glass you would like to test, and then let the test sample cool completely. If the piece hasn't visibly cracked, this means the glass isn't totally incompatible. However, there may still be some stressed areas that aren't yet visible, but will eventually crack.

2. To test the piece further, place it in the freezer for twenty-four hours, and then remove and let it warm to room temperature. Any hidden stress points should reveal themselves.

3. Test the glass combination even further by running the fused sample though a dishwashing cycle. The cold of the freezer followed by the heat of the dishwasher is a great way to test durability; this is especially important for functional pieces that are intended for everyday use.

PREPARING THE KILN FOR FIRING

First and foremost, read the owner's manual. The manufacturer will guide you through the steps in setting up your particular kiln. Generally, you will have to perform a test firing without anything in the kiln, and you may have to make a note of the temperatures that correlate to numbers on the dial. Each kiln is unique; spend time getting to know it and you will be better able to use it successfully.

CLEAN IT OUT

If you've never used your kiln before, you'll need to prepare it for the first firing. It will probably be filled with dust or particles, which can get embedded in glass during firing. It's best to vacuum the interior thoroughly to be sure it's completely clean. Kilns are made of firebrick, a very soft material, so be careful not to damage it when vacuuming.

PROTECT THE KILN SURFACES

Both the kiln floor and the top surface of the kiln shelf will need to be protected so that your glass project doesn't stick to them and so stray bits of glass don't burn into the firebrick. This is accomplished by applying kiln wash or using fiber paper.

- **Fiber paper:** Using scissors, cut it to fit the shape of the kiln shelf, and then fire it to about 1200°F (650°C) to burn off the binder in the paper. Keep the kiln vent open, and make sure the room is well ventilated, as the paper releases an odor. Fiber paper can be reused, so be careful not to rip it when removing it. Always wear protective gloves and a particle mask when handling fiber paper because the fibers shouldn't be inhaled.

- **Kiln wash:** Mix this powder with water according to the manufacturer's directions. The use a paintbrush to apply at least four coats, brushing in a different direction each time. Let the kiln wash dry. When the coating begins to flake off, remove it completely with a paint scraper, vacuum the particles, and then reapply; be sure to wear a particle mask.

LOADING THE KILN

To properly heat glass, air needs to circulate around the piece. For this reason, glass is set on a kiln shelf, which is propped up with kiln posts. These accessories will most likely come with your kiln, along with guidelines for positioning them within your kiln. The kiln shelf needs to be protected with kiln wash or fiber paper as well.

KEEP A FIRING LOG

To repeat your successes and to avoid repeating mistakes, keep a firing log. Some of the things you should record are:

- The technique used: fusing, slumping, or other
- Type of glass used
- What happened to the glass at each temperature stage
- How long the kiln stayed at each temperature
- Whether you used fiber paper or kiln wash
- How often and how long you flash vented

As you gain experience, your firing log will likely become more sophisticated and detailed.

FUSING

There are many things for which your glass-working kiln can be used. Begin the creative journey by becoming familiar with the fusing process described here; then, explore the possibilities.

The process of fusing has five stages. The duration and temperature of each stage depends on the chosen glass, the kiln, and the kind of project you're making.

1. **Heating:** During this stage, glass is heated from room temperature to the fusing point.
2. **Soaking:** During this stage, the kiln is kept at a specific temperature for a period of time to allow the piece to continue to fuse or slump.
3. **Rapid Cooling:** During this stage, the kiln temperature is dropped to just above the annealing temperature range; this is accomplished by flash venting, which involves opening the kiln for a period of time.
4. **Annealing:** During this stage, the fused piece is cooled slowly and becomes solid again.
5. **Final Cooling:** During this stage, the glass has solidified and is allowed to slowly cool to room temperature.

KILNWORKING TERMINOLOGY

- **Fusing:** Pieces of glass are merged together to create a whole.
- **Slumping:** Molds are used to shape glass as it softens to create items such as bowls.
- **Combing:** Tools are used to manipulate the surface of softened glass.
- **Casting:** Small pieces of glass are fused inside a mold. See pages 106-107 for an example.
- **Pate de verre:** Glass "paste" is fused inside a mold.

THE HEATING STAGE

As a kiln reaches certain temperature ranges, the consistency and characteristics of your glass will go through discernable changes. Learning to understand and recognize these specific stages is the key to successful fusing.

Keep in mind that the temperature ranges listed below are approximate; the actual temperature at which a piece of glass reaches a certain stage will depend on the type, shape, and thickness of glass being used. This is one reason why it's important to understand the process and learn to recognize the stages rather than relying on temperatures as guidelines.

1. Room temperature to approximately 1000°F (540°C): Glass remains solid, but begins to expand.
2. 1000°F to 1300°F (540°C to 700°C): The glass begins to soften and look shiny.
3. 1300°F to 1400°F (700°C to 760°C): Glass pieces will begin to stick together; glass slumps fully.
4. 1400°F to 1500°F (760°C to 815°C): Slumped glass may begin to stretch out of shape. Two pieces of glass will become fully fused.
5. 1500°F to 1700°F (815°C to 927°C): Glass becomes molten and will begin to glow red. At around 1700°F (927°C), the glass can be combed. Attempt this only after you become comfortable with fusing and slumping.

SOAKING

Once the kiln reaches the desired temperature, the level of heat is maintained for a period of time before cooling the glass.

The amount of soaking time depends entirely on the effect you want to achieve. A longer soaking time during fusing will cause the glass to spread more, resulting in a smoother, flatter piece. A longer soaking time during slumping will also cause the glass to conform more closely to the mold. Check the progress of your piece and keep good records of the length of time needed to achieve particular effects. The kiln, type of glass, size, and thickness of the piece all have an effect on the soak time.

RAPID COOLING

Once your project has achieved the desired shape, it needs to be cooled quickly to stop any further fusing or slumping. This is achieved by flash venting, which simply involves holding the kiln open for several seconds. Be cautious when doing this, and wear protective gloves.

ANNEALING

Annealing refers to the slow cooling process, when glass gradually hardens. If glass is cooled too quickly, stress points and cracks will occur.

Different glass will anneal at different rates. When you begin, the safest way to cool a piece, especially when combining different glasses, is to do it as slowly as possible. This means minimizing the number of flash vents, keeping the kiln vents plugged, and making sure the room temperature is not too cold. The annealing stage begins when the natural color begins to return to the glass, and the kiln has cooled to approximately 1050°F (565°C).

FINAL COOLING

Once the piece is safely annealed, the final cooling stage begins, at about 750°F (400°C). Don't open the kiln or subject the room to temperature extremes at this point. This may cause the glass to crack.

Keep a record of the time it takes your kiln to cool. Larger pieces may require more time, and if your kiln naturally cools too quickly, try firing the kiln intermittently on a low setting to slow the cooling process.

FUSING STEP BY STEP

There are four major steps to creating a fused project: Cut the glass; load the kiln; fire the kiln; and clean and refine the piece.

1. Cut the glass. Review Cold Glass Basic Techniques on page 8, if necessary. The same techniques and tools apply to cutting glass for fused projects. Take care that the edges of the glass pieces are fairly smooth; any bumps and burrs will create a sloppy fused line. Wash and dry the glass using a lint-free cloth.

2. Load the kiln. Prepare the kiln and shelf using fiber paper or kiln wash. Layer your glass pieces on the kiln shelf; this can be done inside or outside the kiln. Place the shelf in the kiln.

3. Fire the kiln.

   a. Slowly raise the heat to the full fusing temperature indicated by the glass manufacturer.

   b. Soak the glass. Begin by following the guidelines provided by the glass manufacturer, and adjust as needed. Watch the glass carefully to monitor the progress. Refer to Fusing on page 61 if you need to adjust times and temperatures.

   c. Flash vent the kiln to just above 1050°F (565°C) by opening the kiln all the way for approximately eight seconds, and then close the door and check the temperature. Repeat the procedure until the temperature falls below 1100°F (595°C). Use extreme caution when doing this! The heat from the kiln will be intense. If your kiln doesn't automatically turn off when opened, turn it off manually (only while the kiln is open). This is a necessary safety precaution when using electric kilns

   d. Begin annealing the glass when the temperature drops to 1050°F (565°C). Control the rate of temperature decrease to about 3°F (-16°C) per minute. This is a very slow rate, which should work well for just about any glass. Remember—you can anneal too quickly, but not too slowly! To determine your kiln's rate of temperature increase and decrease for each setting, as well as the natural rate of cooling once the kiln is turned off, perform a test run and record the information in your firing log. This information is very helpful during the annealing process.

   e. Turn the kiln off and allow it to cool to room temperature once it reaches 750°F (400°C). Don't open the kiln during this stage.

4. Clean and refine the piece. Once the piece has cooled to room temperature, clean the piece. If you used fiber paper, gently peel it away while wearing gloves and a particle mask. Save it for later use, and then wash the glass. If you used kiln wash, you'll need to clean off any residue that stuck to the glass.

Try to keep the edges of your glass pieces as smooth as possible, like the ones seen here, if you want to maintain clean lines in the finished piece.

To smooth any rough edges, use a metal file, sandpaper, or an electric grinder (available from stained glass suppliers). To further refine rough edges, you may want to re-fire the piece to about 1200°F (650°C) to round the rough edges after filing or sanding them.

If your piece has unwanted bubbles or cracks, you've most likely fired the piece too quickly. Try slowing down different stages of the process, and keep records of how the glass reacts. This way, you'll discover exactly where the trouble lies and be able to consistently avoid it.

SLUMPING

Now that you understand the fusing process, try slumping—using a mold to shape glass. The firing process is the same as fusing, except that the optimum temperature for slumping is lower that the fusing point. The general range for slumping is about 1000°F to 1400°F (540°C to 760°C). So, if you want a slumped piece to have fused elements, you will need to do the fusing first. Then, refire the piece using a mold.

The actual temperature at which you reach the desired slumping effect will depend on the glass, kiln, and size of the piece. The slumping projects in this book call for Spectrum System 96™ glass; if you use it, you can follow the given temperature guidelines with confidence until you become more comfortable with the process.

SLUMPING OVER A MOLD
Slumping over stainless steel molds works best because steel contracts more than glass—which means it won't push into and interfere with the glass while it is slumping. Slumping over a mold creates beautiful draped folds.

SLUMPING INTO A MOLD
If you want to create a nicely round bowl or platter, allow the glass to slump into the mold. To prepare a mold for this technique, drill small holes in the bottom to allow the air to escape, or purchase a mold specifically designed for the task. Once you're ready to use the mold, cover the inside with several layers of kiln wash.

SELECTING A MOLD

Fusing suppliers offer commercial molds, but you can also make your own. Below are some of the materials that can be safely used as molds.

- **Stainless steel:** Lightweight, durable, and sturdy, stainless steel makes an ideal form. Simply coat it with a few layers of kiln wash. Try raiding kitchen supply stores for an inexpensive array of bowl molds. Because of the rate of expansion as compared to glass, it is best for slumping over.
- **Clay:** Slumping into pottery works well, once the surface is covered with a few layers of kiln wash. Because of the rate of expansion as compared to glass, it is best or slumping into.
- **Found items:** Tin cans, rocks, cement, and other items that can withstand the heat of the kiln can make interesting molds. Just coat with kiln wash, and test the piece in the kiln by slowly raising the heat (without any glass)to see how it behaves. This will also burn off any water or superficial residue that would interfere with slumping.
- **Ceramic fiber material:** Look for moldable ceramic fiber products from your kiln supplier. It can be shaped similar to the way papier-mâché is used.

Chapter 4

FUSING
AND SLUMPING

In this chapter, you'll find projects to help you get acquainted with basic warm glass techniques. The first two projects, the Fern Plate on page 68 and the Organic Tiles on page 72, will guide you through the fusing process; the last two projects, the Art Glass Display Bowl on page 76 and the Fluted Candlestick on page 80, will introduce you to slumping techniques.

Once you become comfortable with the fusing process, you'll be amazed at the wonderful combinations of color and texture you can achieve by mixing and matching glass. Don't be afraid to experiment—it's the best way to learn and discover Just be sure to follow the appropriate safety precautions.

If you've never fused glass or operated a kiln before, begin with a small fusing project before attempting a slumping project. To slump successfully, it's crucial to know your kiln and to be able to recognize the stages that glass goes through as it's heated. Don't worry—this won't take long!

Fern Plate

This project is a great way to learn how to illustrate using glass pieces. One of the most fascinating aspects of fusing is the way in which different glass merges to create interesting effects and colors. On this plate, a slight halo of darker green emerged around the fern elements, creating the illusion of depth. When designing a piece such as this one, keep in mind that glass spreads out a little when heated. This can be desirable or not—it depends on the look you're trying to achieve.

MATERIALS

- Basic fused glass tools and supplies (see page 58)

- 1 sheet of Spectrum System 96 fusing glass for the base, 12" x 12" (30 cm x 30 cm)

- 1/2 sheet of Spectrum System 96™ fusing glass for the fern design, 6" x 12" (15 cm x 30 cm)

DESIGNER'S TIP

Use a small dab of white glue to hold loose glass pieces in place when transporting a project to the kiln. Wait until the glue is tacky before positioning the pieces. Or simply layer the project in the kiln.

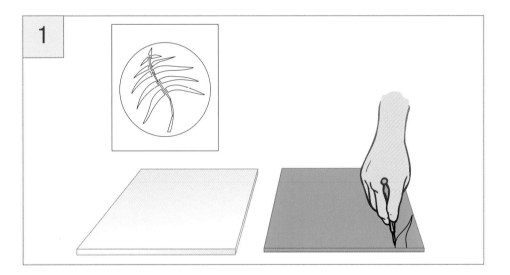

1. CUT, WASH, AND DRY THE GLASS PIECES. Photocopy and cut out the pattern pieces (see page 118). Score and break the glass as closely as possible to the edge of the pattern pieces; try to make the cuts as clean as possible. Groze the edges of the glass gently, if needed. Use a metal file or sandpaper to refine the edges of the pieces so that there aren't any outstanding bumps. Also try using a Dremel MiniMite fitted with a fine grinding tip for the smoothest finish.

Wash and dry the glass pieces, making sure they are free of lint or fingerprints.

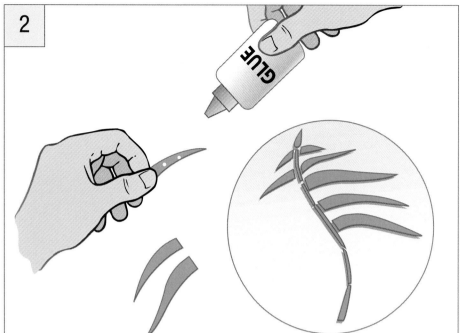

2. ARRANGE THE GLASS PIECES ACCORDING TO THE PATTERN. Layer the glass pieces as desired. Keep in mind that the pieces will spread about $^1/_{16}$" to $^1/_8$" (1.5 mm to 3 mm) when fused. To keep the elements of the design distinct, be sure to arrange the pieces at least $^1/_{16}$" to $^1/_8$" (1.5 mm to 3 mm) apart, or farther apart if you don't want the pieces to touch.

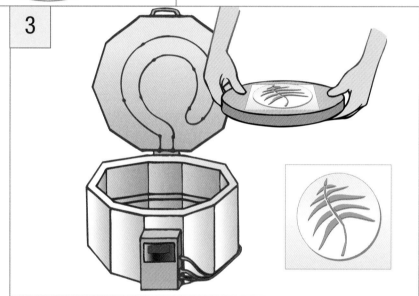

3. FUSE THE PIECE. Prepare and load the kiln as described on page 63. Turn the kiln on high with the vent open. Let it reach the manufacturer's specified fusing temperature for the glass. Carefully open the kiln and check the glass. If it is fused as desired, and then flash vent the kiln by opening the lid all the way for about eight seconds. If not, let the piece fire for a little longer, checking often.

After flash venting, turn off the kiln and plug the vents to soak the piece.

When the kiln temperature reaches 1000°F to 1100°F (540°C to 595°C), flash vent again, this time opening the lid only halfway for about four seconds. Let the kiln cool to room temperature for six to eight hours.

4. CLEAN AND FINISH THE PIECE. Clean the kiln paper or kiln wash residue off the piece. Then, file, sand, or use a Dremel MiniMite fitted with a fine grinding tip to smooth the edges.

TRADE SECRETS

Sometimes glass takes on a whitish, dull surface appearance with spots after being fired. This is one reason for the rapid cooling stage (see Fusing, page 61), which minimizes the amount of time spent in the devitrification temperature range of 1100°F to 1400°F (595°C to 760°C). You may or may not like the effect—some artists like the effect, whereas others try to avoid it.

To help prevent devitrification, use an overspray (or devit spray). Some sprays damage iridescent coatings on glass, so fire the piece with the iridescent side face down, and use the spray on the other side of the glass.

Complex designs can benefit from differences in the finish.

Organic Tiles

Layer flowers and foliage between two pieces of glass for striking, naturalistic designs. Here, we used fan-shaped gingko leaves of different sizes to make the white and green tiles and pink hydrangea blossoms to make the blue tile. The effect is an organic, fossil-like look. Experiment with different kinds of materials; each one will have a unique effect. However, you can count on the same material to produce the same look again and again.

MATERIALS

Makes 2 tiles:

- Basic fused glass tools and supplies (see page 58)

- ½ sheet of colored Spectrum System 96 fusing glass, 6" x 12" (15 cm x 30 cm)

- ½ sheet of clear fusing glass, 6" x 12" (15 cm x 30 cm)

- Dried and pressed leaves and flowers

DESIGNER'S TIP

Press your own flowers and leaves by placing them in the pages of an old telephone book. Lay more books on top to add more weight, if needed.

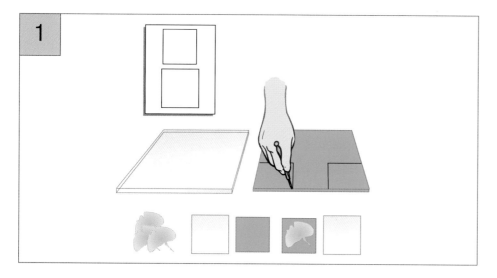

1. CUT, WASH, AND DRY THE GLASS PIECES. Photocopy and cut out the pattern pieces (see page 119). Score and break the glass as closely as possible to the edge of the pattern pieces; try to make the cuts as clean as possible. Groze the edges of the glass gently, if needed. Use a metal file or sandpaper to refine the edges of the pieces so that there aren't any outstanding bumps. Also try using a Dremel MiniMite fitted with a fine grinding tip for the smoothest finish.

Wash and dry the glass pieces, making sure they are free of lint or fingerprints.

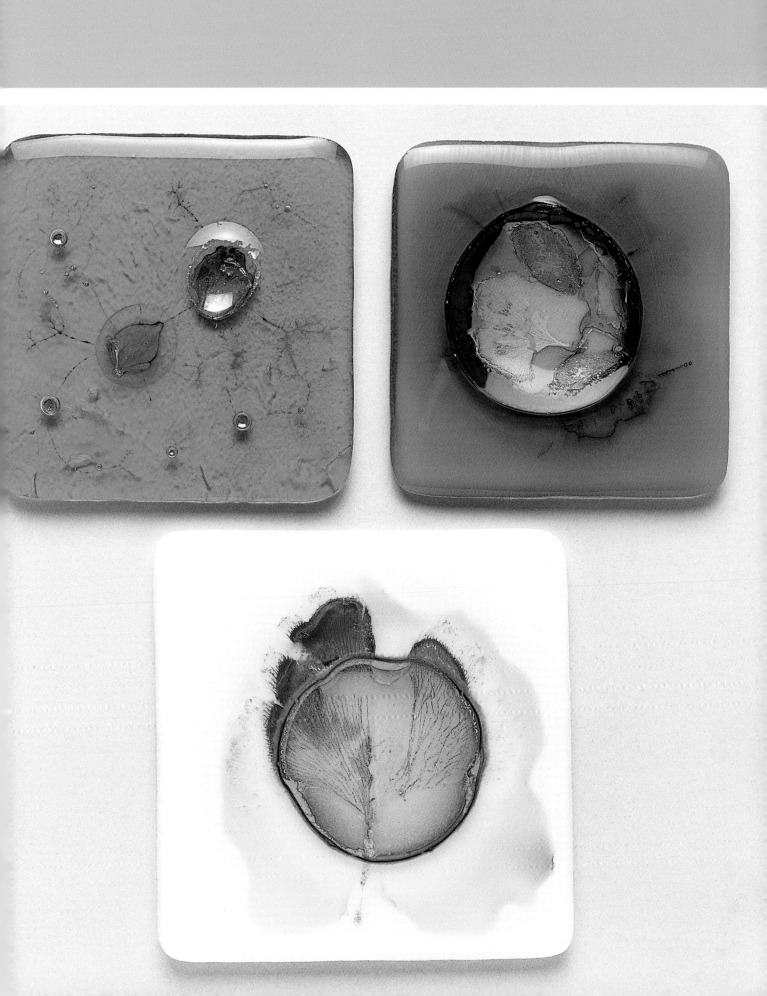

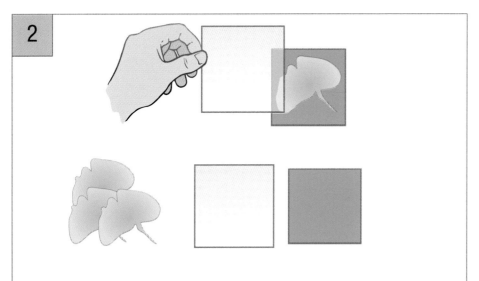

2. ARRANGE THE GLASS PIECES AND THE FOLIAGE AS DESIRED. Layer the foliage on top of the colored glass. Place the slightly larger clear glass on top. The overlap will slump and fuse to the bottom piece, creating smooth, rounded edges. Keep in mind that the embedded material will create a depression in the glass, which will be concentrated toward the center of the foliage.

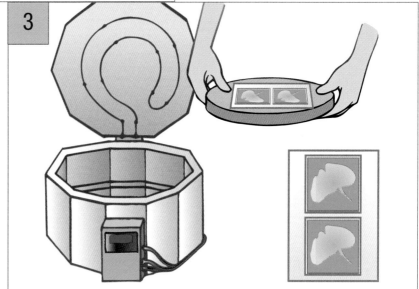

3. FUSE THE TILES. Prepare and load the kiln as described on page 63. Turn the kiln on high with the vent open. Calculate fifteen minutes per tile, and let the kiln fire for this amount of time. Then carefully open the kiln and check the tiles. The foliage should be ashen, and the glass should form a bubble over it. If it hasn't, let the tiles fire for a little longer, checking often. Then plug the vent. Let it reach about 50°F (10°C) above the manufacturer's specified fusing temperature for the glass.

Continue firing the tiles. After about twenty minutes, the temperature should be about 1700°F (926°C); the glass should be molten and glowing red. At this point, flash vent the kiln by opening the lid all the way for about eight seconds. Remove the plug from the vent.

Flash vent every twenty minutes until the kiln temperature reaches 1000°F (540°C), but open the lid only halfway for about four seconds. Let the kiln cool to room temperature for six to eight hours. After the kiln reaches 1000°F (540°C), do not open again until cooled to room temperature.

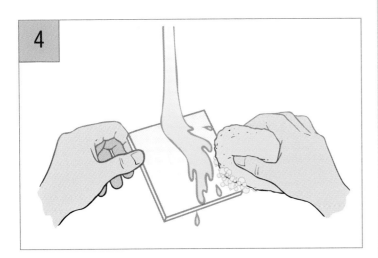

4. CLEAN AND FINISH THE PIECE. Clean the kiln paper or kiln wash residue off the piece. Then, file, sand, or use a Dremel MiniMite fitted with a fine grinding tip to smooth the edges.

TRADE SECRETS

Kiln fiber paper leaves a textured imprint on glass, and the area will have a more matte finish. Many artists use this to their advantage by cutting shapes out of kiln paper and positioning them strategically on the surface of the project, or by sandwiching them between layers of glass.

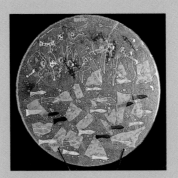

To create fish and seaweed shapes, the artist used cut pieces of kiln paper between two layers of glass, then fused the piece.

Art Glass Display Bowl

This elegant bowl seems to glow with inner light. Luminous amber-colored glass complements the free-form shape, giving the piece a natural, earthy look. Make your own by simply laying a circle of glass over a mold, such as a humble stainless steel mixing bowl that may be hidden away in a cupboard. If the piece doesn't come out the way you'd like, try refiring it.

MATERIALS

- Basic fused glass tools and supplies (see page 58)

- One full sheet of Spectrum System 96 fusing glass, 12" x 12" (30 cm x 30 cm)

- Stainless steel mold (see Selecting a Mold, page 65)

DESIGNER'S TIP

Glass doesn't always slump the way you'd like. When this happens, use a metal skewer or similar tool to gently shape the flutes or drape of a project before cooling the piece.

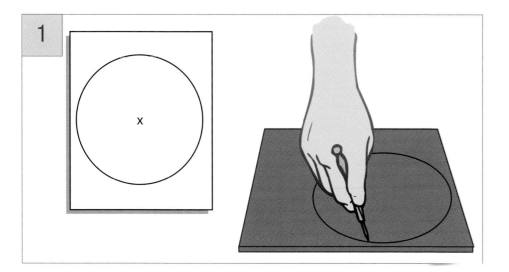

1. CUT, WASH, AND DRY THE GLASS. Photocopy and cut out the pattern (see page 120). Score and break the glass as closely as possible to the edge of the pattern pieces; try to make the cuts as clean as possible. Groze the edges of the glass gently, if needed. Use a metal file or sandpaper to refine the edges of the pieces so that there aren't any outstanding bumps. Also try using a Dremel MiniMite fitted with a fine grinding tip for the smoothest finish.

Wash and dry the glass pieces, making sure they are free of lint or fingerprints.

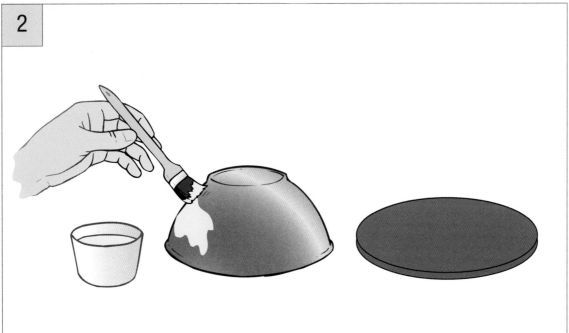

2. PREPARE THE MOLD. Find the center of the glass circle, and mark it by scratching the point with a knife or similar tool.

Prepare the mold by covering it with several layers of kiln wash (see also page 64). Lay the glass circle on the mold, making sure that the center point is aligned over the top of the mold.

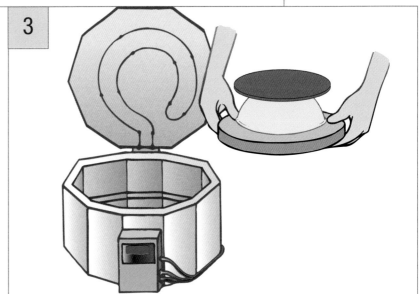

3. SLUMP THE GLASS. Prepare the kiln as described on page 63. Place the glass and mold in the center of the kiln. Turn the kiln on to a setting that corresponds to approximately 1250°F (677°C), with the vent open. When the temperature reaches 1000°F (540°C), carefully open the kiln and check the glass. It should begin to droop over the mold. When the kiln reaches 1100°F to 1150°F (595°C to 620°C), it will begin slumping.

Check often until the bowl reaches the desired look. When it does, turn off the kiln and flash vent by opening the lid all the way for about eight seconds. Put the plug halfway into the vent; you don't want to soak the piece after the desired amount of slumping is achieved. Let the kiln cool to room temperature for six to eight hours.

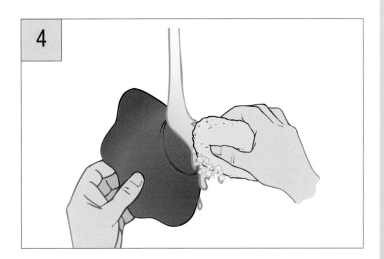

4. CLEAN AND FINISH THE PIECE. Clean the kiln paper or kiln wash residue off the piece. Then, file, sand, or use a Dremel MiniMite fitted with a fine grinding tip to smooth the edges.

TRADE SECRETS

As you gain experience in fusing and slumping, you'll begin to discover ways to guide the glass into doing want you want. This knowledge comes from observing the way glass behaves. For instance, the folds that occur in a slumped piece seem to be random—but you can control them to a great extent.

As a piece slumps, any heavier areas fall first. Take advantage of this by cutting or grozing scallops or other designs into perimeter of the glass circle; the areas where glass is taken away will tend to fall after the others. Alternatively, try adding fused decorations to certain areas of the circle. Then, when refiring it over or in a mold, these heavier fused areas will slump first.

Fluted Candlestick

This project involves carving your own mold from soft firebrick. Don't worry—it's much easier than it sounds (see Trade Secrets, page 83). The fabriclike folds created by slumping over a mold add to the graceful beauty of a lit taper candle. The amount of folding corresponds directly to the width of the mold. The wider the mold, the less dramatic the folds will be; the narrower the mold, the more pronounced the folds will be.

MATERIALS

- Basic fused glass tools and supplies (see page 58)

- One full sheet of Spectrum System 96 fusing glass, 12" x 12" (30 cm x 30 cm)

- Mold suitable for firing (see Selecting a Mold, page 65)

DESIGNER'S TIP

When slumping over a mold, choose or make a form that isn't overly complex or detailed and one that is wider at the top than the bottom. You want to be sure that you can remove the glass easily once the piece has cooled.

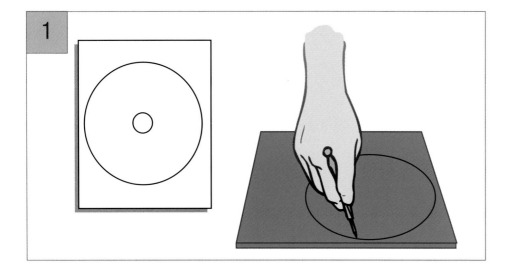

1. CUT, WASH, AND DRY THE GLASS. Photocopy and cut out the pattern (see page 121). Score and break the glass as closely as possible to the edge of the pattern pieces; try to make the cuts as clean as possible. Groze the edges of the glass gently, if needed. Use a metal file or sandpaper to refine the edges of the pieces so that there aren't any outstanding bumps. Also try using a Dremel MiniMite fitted with a fine grinding tip for the smoothest finish.

Wash and dry the glass pieces, making sure they are free of lint or fingerprints.

2. PREPARE THE MOLD. Find the center of the glass circle, and mark it by scratching the point with a knife or similar tool.

Prepare the mold by covering it with several layers of kiln wash (also see pages 64–65). Lay the glass circle on the mold, making sure that the center point is aligned over the top of the mold. To make the mold used for this project, see Trade Secrets, opposite.

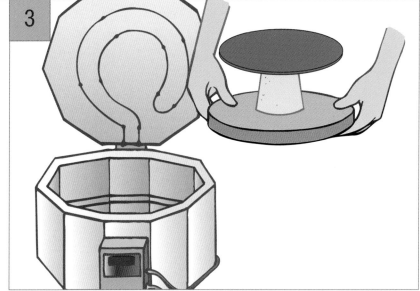

3. SLUMP THE GLASS. Prepare the kiln as described on page 63. Place the glass and mold in the center of the kiln. Turn the kiln on to a setting that corresponds to approximately 1250°F (677°F), with the vent open. When the temperature reaches 1000°F (540°C), carefully open the kiln and check the glass. It should begin to droop over the mold. When the kiln reaches 1100°F to 1150°F (595°C to 620°C), it will begin slumping.

Check often until the candlestick reaches the desired look. When it does, turn off the kiln and flash vent by opening the lid all the way for about eight seconds. Put the plug halfway into the vent; you don't want to soak the piece after the desired amount of slumping is achieved. Let the kiln cool to room temperature for six to eight hours.

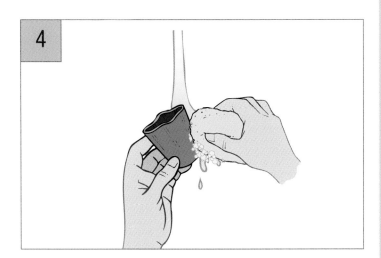

4. CLEAN AND FINISH THE PIECE. Clean the kiln paper or kiln wash residue off the piece. Then, file, sand, or use a Dremel MiniMite fitted with a fine grinding tip to smooth the edges.

TRADE SECRETS

Soft, lightweight firebrick makes a great mold for slumping because it is easily carved with an ordinary serrated knife. Imagine the possibilities—you are not limited to store-bought molds!

To carve a tapered mold to make the candlestick seen here, begin with a piece of firebrick about 2" x 4" (5 cm x 10 cm). Refine the shape using a knife and finally sandpaper. The finished dimensions should be about 1" (2.5 cm) at top, 1 1/2" (4 cm) at the base, and about 3" (8 cm) high. This will make a mold suitable for the 7" (18 cm) circle of glass used in this project. To be sure that the finished piece is level on a table top, smooth and flatten the corresponding area on the mold until it rests.

Kilns are made of firebrick and come with firebrick accessories, so firebrick is readily available at any kiln supplier in various shapes and sizes.

Try making your own mask molds using firebrick.

Chapter 5

CONTINUING
THE JOURNEY

Now that you have learned the basics, let this gallery of artwork inspire you to expand your know-how. From traditional painting to kiln casting, the world of art glass is diverse and exciting. You'll get a taste of myriad styles of modern glass art—and a hint of what you can create yourself—from each of the talented artists whose work you will encounter on the following pages. Remember, you can go as far as you want; don't be intimidated by more advanced techniques. Everyone starts at the beginning.

To continue the journey, look to professional organizations, trade periodicals, and local suppliers for information on classes and communities of glass artists (see Resources, page 122). No matter how long you've been doing something, there's always something new to discover. Experienced artisans can learn as much from novices as novices can learn from them—a fresh perspective can be both invigorating and enlightening. This exchange is the lifeblood of art.

May your glass always break in an interesting (if unintentional) way!

Gallery of Art Glass

Giorgetta McRee, United States

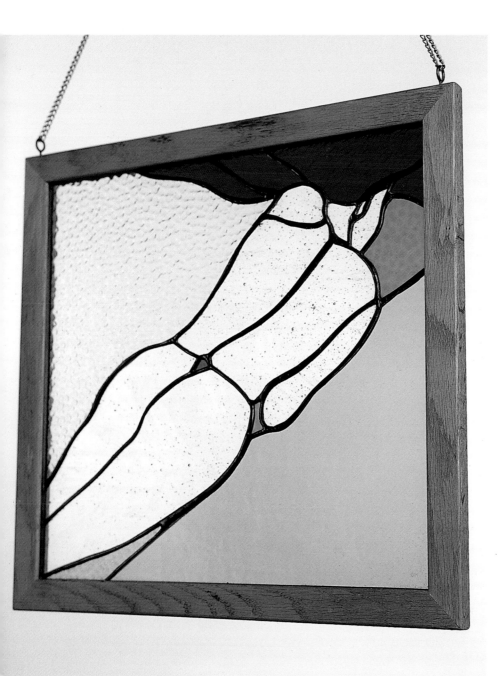

Creating a picture with pieces of glass isn't only about color and shape. Glass often has embossed texture, like the sand seen here. The textured side is technically the back, but that doesn't mean you can't use it as the front!

Uriel. Sheets of glass have uneven, fluid-looking edges, which don't have to be trimmed away. One such edge inspired the face in this piece.

This holiday wreath is accented with glass drop jewels, which have a flat back. They are available in many colors and sizes and are an easy way to incorporate round, dimensional shapes into a stained glass piece.

Lamps are coveted stained glass pieces because of their elegance and grace. Kits, which include bases, frames, and wiring, are available from stained glass suppliers. In this lamp, opaque glass is used at the bottom and translucent glass is used at the top, which causes the light to diffuse upward.

Lit pieces don't always have to be lamp shades. The shell, which is translucent, makes a perfect focal point.

This lighted cube is a prime example of the intricate, mosaiclike detail that can be achieved with the copper-foil method. In traditional stained glass, these details would have to be painted.

Jessy Carrara, United States

The dragonfly components of these earrings and necklace are made of dichroic glass. The wings are clear glass, but the dichroic film on the surface makes them glisten and appear colored. The body is accordion glass, which has ridges that are reminiscent of a real dragonfly's body. The pieces are fused in one firing.

Like the dragonflies, these turtles are also made of dichroic glass. They are made by first fusing the patchwork accents to the turtle's back. Then, the head and legs are added in a second firing.

Andrea and Brian Scholes, United States

These pins are fused just enough to attach the glass pieces, so that the dimensional quality remains. Gold leaf accents fired on the surface of some are another way to add eye-catching details.

Photographer: Jim Padilla

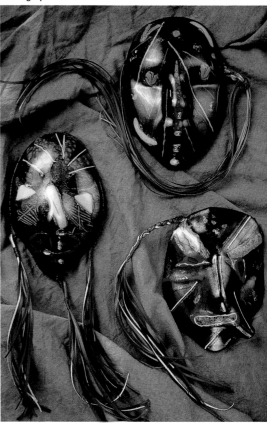

These fused masks incorporate ribbon and some sandblasted details. The combination of textures, colors, and dimension create tactile, visceral designs.

This piece is appropriately entitled *Underwater Fantasy*. The scene was sandwiched between two layers of glass and then fired. The design consists of copper, brass, and gold leaf and dichroic glass. To create the ghost images, the artist cut kiln fiber paper into fish and seaweed shapes.

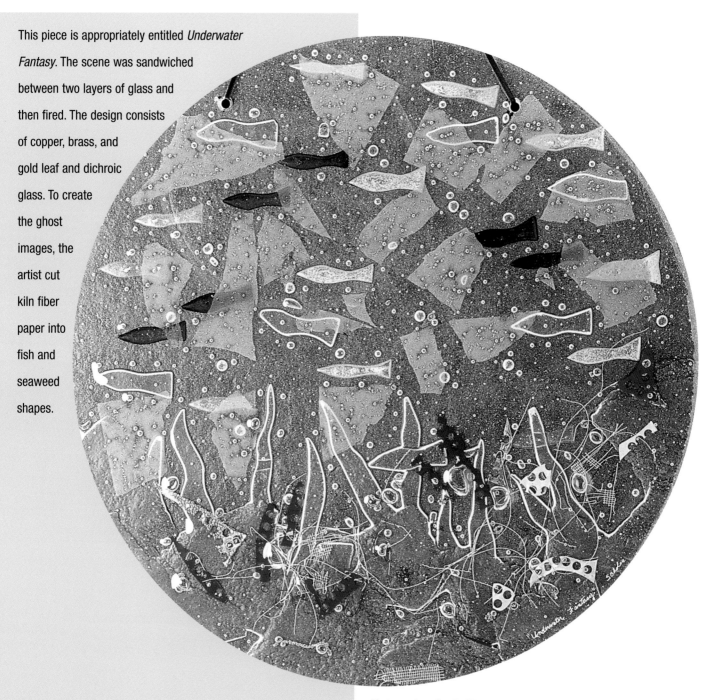

Photographer: Jim Padilla

This fused and slumped bowl features a lively, bold design. By layering the underside extensively with pieces of kiln fiber paper, the artist added textured impressions, which are created when the glass melts around the paper during fusing.

Photographer: Jim Padilla

The gorgeous beadwork on this sumptuous box accentuates the openwork pattern on the lid. The organic, detailed design comes almost entirely from the soldered elements.

Crystals and gemstones are a perfect choice for adorning glass art because of their inherent luminosity, and often, translucency. The beads and gems on this box and kaleidoscope seem to grow naturally from the soldering.

Urban Man, 2000. The joyous figure seen at left was created using lacquer paint on ¹/₂" (1 cm) plate glass. The glass is sandblasted and has grozed edges.

Mambo, 2000. This couple was created entirely by sandblasting on ¹/₂" (1 cm) plate glass; the edges are grozed.

Shaman Mask, 1999. The untamed raffia accents on this brightly colored fused glass mask give it a primitive vigor. Combining glass with strikingly different materials can yield exciting, energetic pieces.

Arte en Vidrio, Mexico

Eng. Raul Urbina Torres, Mrs. Leticia Martínez de Urbina, and Mrs. Rosario Lopéz Balam

The artistic possibilities of fusing are readily apparent in this array of pendants. The pieces seen here have been fused with a variety of materials, including sand, silver, copper, and gold.

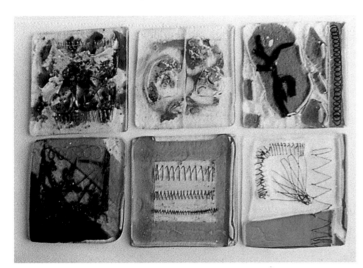

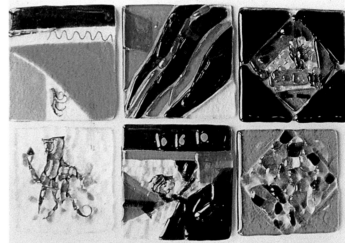

Fused tiles make striking architectural elements. Some of the ones shown above are not fully fused to retain some dimension. Imagine a mosaic made with custom tiles—the potential for illustrative work is exciting!

This Moroccan-style house in Mérida city is a breathtaking example of classic glass art. The artists of Arte en Vidrio who restored the beauty of the glasswork involved many techniques, including etching and high-fire painting.

The arched installation seen here is an example of traditional stained glass. The details are painted on large pieces of glass, creating a refined and classic work.

Eng. Raul Urbina Torres, Mrs. Leticia Martínez de Urbina, and Mrs. Rosario Lopéz Balam

The two photographs shown above are more examples of traditional stained glass, as the details are painted. Notice the heavier dark lines, which indicate where the glass pieces are joined together. They follow the graceful curves of the design so as not to detract from the image.

Religion has inspired much of the world's greatest art. The window installations in this church are examples of innovative, modern glass art depicting the stations of crucifixion.

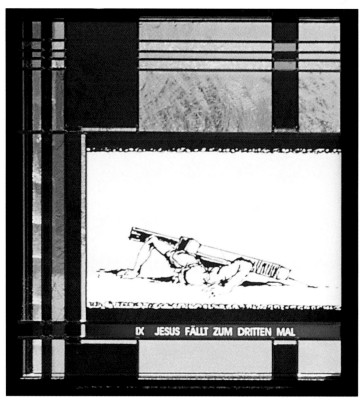

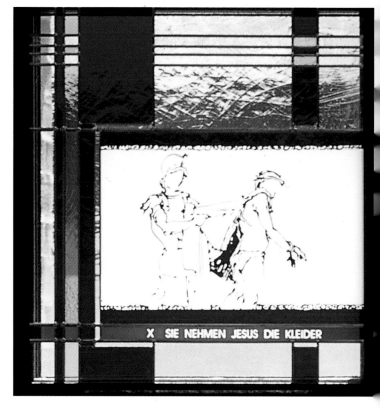

Detail: Jesus is being taken off the cross. The artist created these intricate illustrations by drawing them on antique blue glass using wood glue. Once the glue had dried, the rest of the glass was sandblasted to create the white space. Then, the glue was washed off, revealing the blue design.

Detail: Jesus is put to the grave.

Paar. This sculpture was kiln cast, a technique that involves melting glass within a mold. Additional details were cut into the piece.

Stay. This sculpture involved a variety of techniques: casting, pouring molten glass, cutting, and sandblasting.

Anja Isphording, Canada

This vessels are made of kiln cast lead crystal, which was then cut and polished. The artist used the lost wax technique, which involves sculpting wax. This allowed her to create the fluid, curving details in the finished piece.

Glass, usually thought of as a rigid, cold material, can take on an amazing warmth and organic texture when sculpted in this manner—proving the amazing artistic versatility of glass and glass artists.

The vessels on both pages were both kiln cast using the lost wax technique. Both are reminiscent of delicate sea anemones, a look that surprises and delights when created with glass.

PATTERNS

All the projects in this book have an accompanying pattern. They are presented on the following pages. The percentage shown below each pattern indicates whether a pattern has been reduced or enlarged. If the pattern is not shown actual size, you'll need to enlarge or reduce accordingly to attain the correct size or the dimensions of the piece. However, with a photocopier, you can easily reduce or enlarge the pattern to suit your needs. See Preparing Patterns on page 10. Also, if a required pattern is a simple shape (such as a plain square with no ornamentation or added elements), we have only provided measurements for those patterns (for example, a 5" by 5" [13 cm by 13 cm] square that will act as the bottom of a candleholder). You'll need to measure and cut out the pattern on a sturdy piece of paper or thin cardboard (such as a manila folder).

Patterns are easy to design yourself once you learn the basics of stained glass assembly. Similar to a mosaic, pattern pieces must fit together like a puzzle. Once you get to know glass, you'll soon realize that soldering lines have to be placed in certain areas of a design out of necessity. Learn to use these restrictions in creative ways, adjusting your original design if needed. Remember, soldered seams are as much a part of the design as the shapes and colors of the glass.

You'll also quickly discover what kind of pieces are difficult to cut and which are easier. In the beginning, try to avoid the temptation to create difficult patterns that would be frustrating for a novice to construct; you'll only end up getting discouraged, though with some practice, you'll be able to make that window-sized landscape! Once you understand what makes a successful pattern, you'll be able to convert any image to glass, from photographs to paintings.

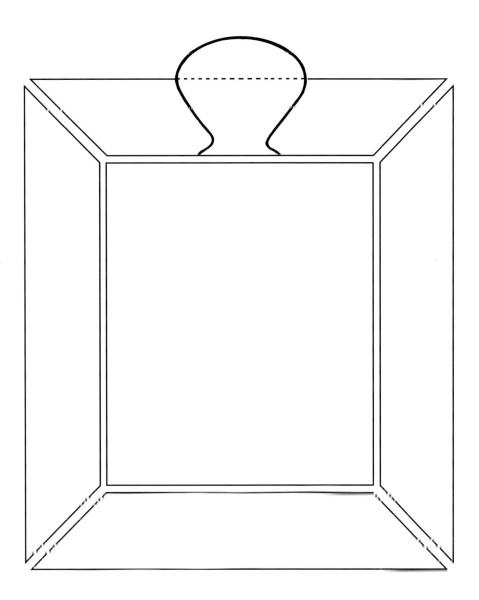

Mermaid Mirror, page 18
(shown at 50%)

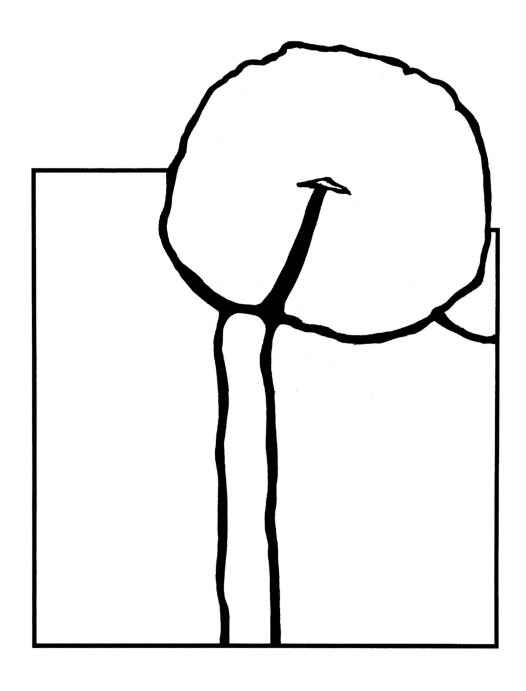

FRONT

BACK
Cut out three squares measuring 5" x 5" (13 cm x 13 cm) for the
two sides and the bottom.

Geode Candleholder, page 22
(shown at 100%)

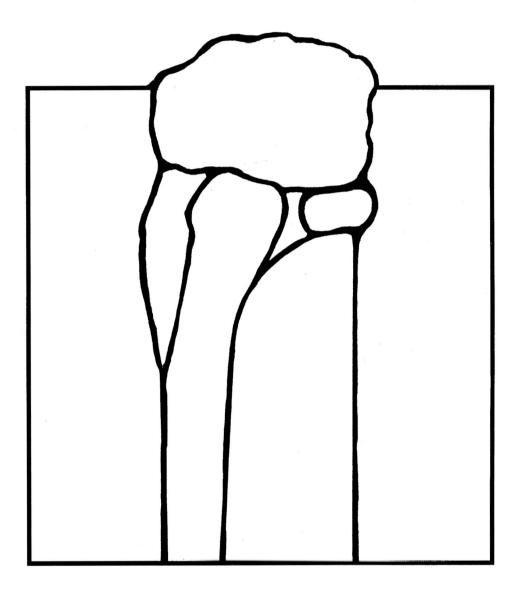

BACK

Trinket Tray, page 26
(shown at 100%)

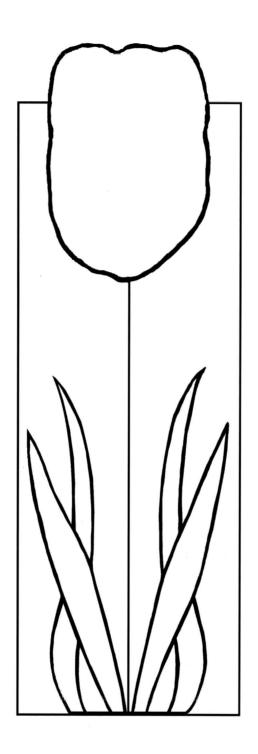

SIDES
Cut three 8" x 3" (20 cm x 8 cm) rectangles for the sides.

DOTTOM
Cut one 3" x 3" (8 om x 8 om) oquare for the bottom.

Tulip Vase, page 32
(shown at 80%)

FRONT/BACK

CUT 2

BOTTOM

Art Deco Napkin Holder, page 36
(shown at 100%)

Mooncatcher, page 40
(shown at 100%)

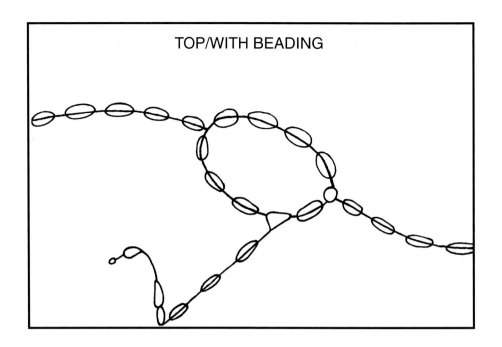

TOP/WITH BEADING

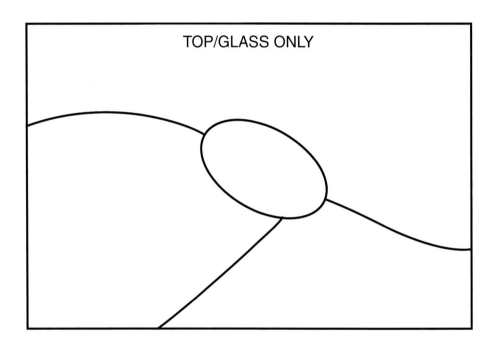

TOP/GLASS ONLY

FRONT AND BACK SIDES
Cut two 1½" x 6" (4 cm x 15 cm) rectangles for the front and back sides.

LEFT AND RIGHT SIDES
Cut two 1½" x 4" (4 cm x 10 cm) rectangles for the left and right sides.

BOTTOM
Cut two 4" x 5¾" (10 cm x 15 cm) rectangles for the bottom.

Cabochon Jewelry Box, page 46
(shown at 80%)

Bird in Flight, page 50
(shown at 100%)

FRONT

BOTTOM

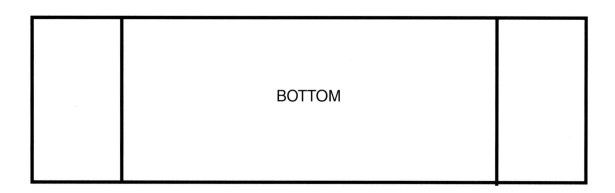

BACK

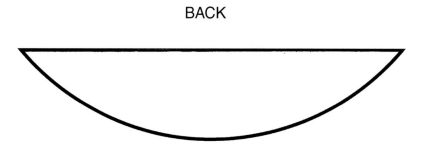

Tree Tea Light, page 54
(shown at 100%)

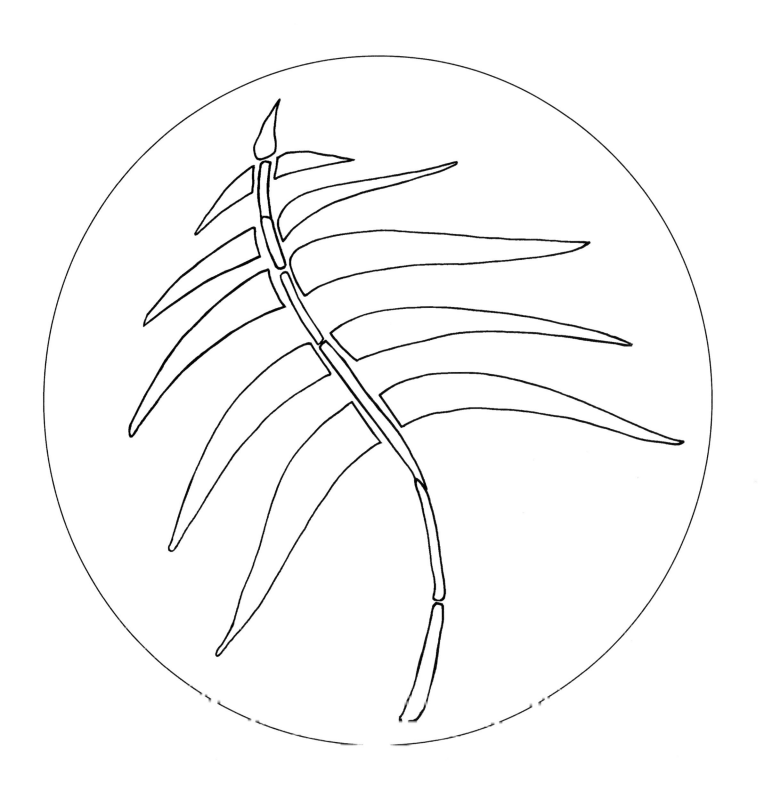

Fern Plate, page 68
(shown at 80%)

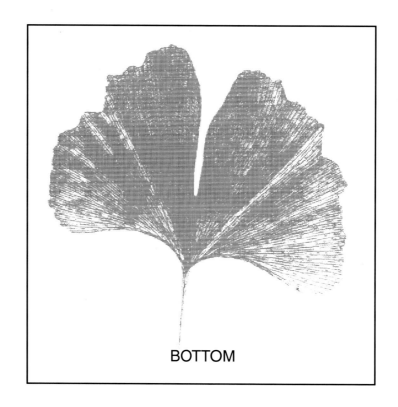

BOTTOM

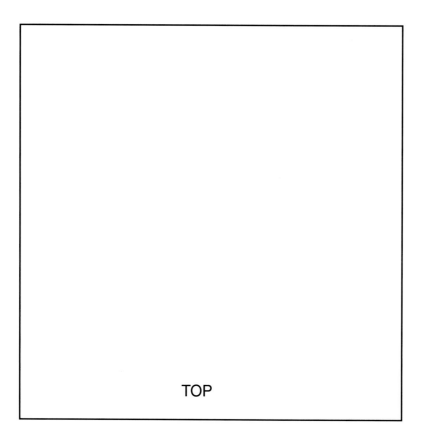

TOP

Organic Tiles, page 72
(shown at 100%)

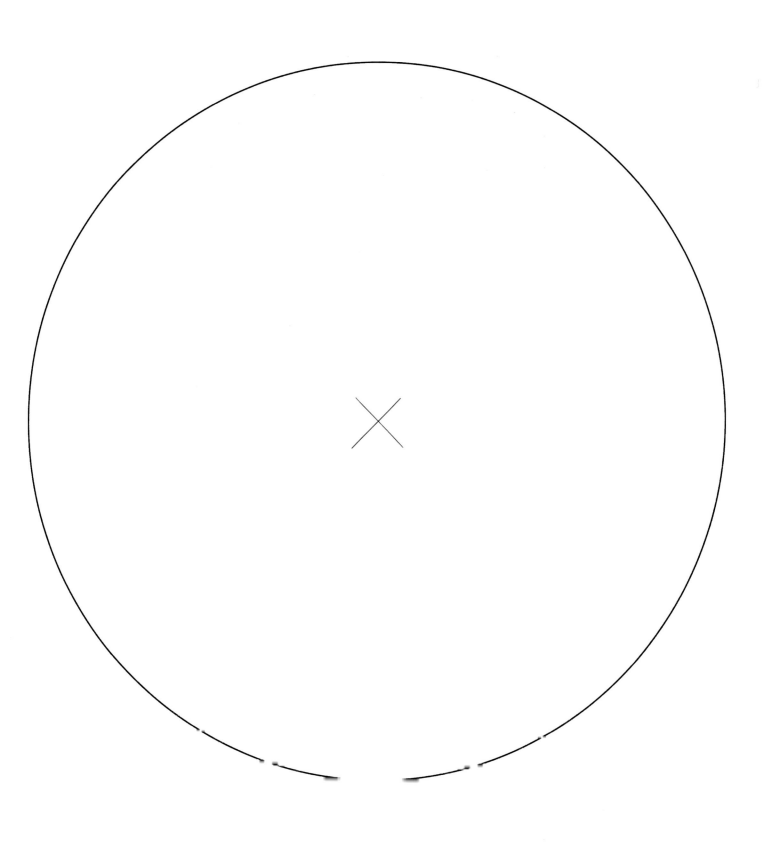

Art Glass Display Bowl, page 76
(shown at 100%)

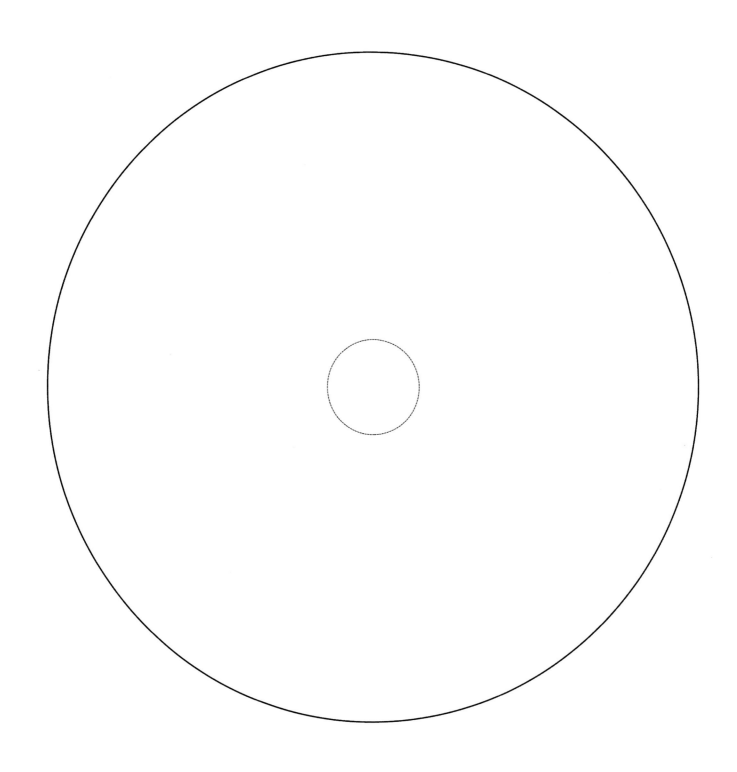

Fluted Candlestick, page 80
(shown at 100%)

Resources

Stained Glass and Fusing Supplies

Albion Glass and Mirror
P.O. Box 27
Albion Q 4010, Australia
Phone: (07) 3862 6227
Fax: (07) 3262 7605
E-mail: help@albionglass.com.au
Web site: www.albionglass.com.au
Stained glass supplies; offers courses and workshops

B & B Etching Products
19721 N. 98th Avenue
Peoria, AZ 85382, USA
Phone: USA, (888) 382-425;
International, (803) 584-7315
Fax: (803) 584-7316
E-mail: etchall@etchall.com
Web site: www.etchall.com
Etching creme and supplies; order custom adhesive vinyl stencils from your sketches for a small fee

Centre DeVerre
18 Bartlett Street
Allenstown, NH 03275, USA
Phone: (800) 958-5319; (603) 485-8344
Fax: (603) 485-2444
E-mail: service@cdvkiln.com
Web site: www.cdvkiln.com
Kilns and kiln accessories; glass paints

Delphi Stained Glass
3380 East Jolly Road
Lansing, MI 48910, USA
Phone: (800) 248-2048; (517) 394-4631
Fax: (000) 740 0071; (517) 394 6764
E-mail: sales@delphiglass.com
Web site: www.delphiglass.com
Stained glass and fusing supplies

Fantasy In Glass
703 The Queensway
Toronto, ON M8Y 1L2, Canada
Phone: (416) 252-0000
Fax: (416) 252-8915
Toll Free: (800) 841-5758
Web site: www.fantasyinglass.com
Stained glass supplies; some fusing supplies

Glass Crafters Stained Glass, Inc.
398 Interstate Court
Sarasota, FL 34240, USA
Phone: Orders, (800) 422-4552; Customer Service, (941) 379-8333
Fax: (941) 379-8827
E-mail: info@glasscrafters.com
Web site: www.glasscrafters.com
Stained glass and fusing supplies

Hee Sun Stained Glass, Ltd.
324 Main Street
Reisterstown, MD 21136, USA
Phone: (888) 508-5595; (410) 833-3007
E-mail: sales@heesun.com
Web site: www.heesun.com/catalog.html
Stained glass supplies; some fusing supplies

HobbyCraft *(stores throughout the UK)*
Head office
Bournemouth
Phone: 01202 596 100
Supplies glass paint and glass work tools

Hot Glass Horizons
15500 NE Kincaid Road
Newberg, OR 97132, USA
Phone: (503) 538-5281
Fax: (503) 538-6527
E-mail: glaswiz@aol.com
Web site: www.hotglasshorizons.com
Fusing supplies

Hot Glass Supply
E-mail: sales@hotglasssupply.com
Web site: www.hotglasssupply.com
Sells Spectrum System 96 glass for fusing and kilns

James Hetley & Co. Ltd.
Glasshouse Fields, Stepney
London E1W 3JA, UK
Phone: (0)20-7790-2333
Fax: (0)20-7790-0201
Web site: www.hetleys.co.uk
Stained glass supplies; some fusing supplies

Kansa Craft
The Old Flour Mill
Wath Road
Elsecar
Barnsley
S Yorks S74 8HW, England
Phone: 01226 747 424

Lead & Light
35a Hartland Road
London NW1 4DB, England
Phone: 0207 485 0997

Skutt Kilns
6441 S.E. Johnson Creek Boulevard
Portland, OR 97206, USA
Phone: (503) 774-6000
Fax: (503) 774-7833
E-mail: skutt@skutt.com
Web site: www.skutt.com

Stained Glass Warehouse, Inc.
P.O. Box 609
Arden, NC 28704, USA
Phone: (828) 687-1057
Fax: (828) 684-8861
Email: info@stainedglasswarehouse.com
Web site: www.stainedglasswarehouse.com
Stained glass and fusing supplies; kilns

Tempsford Stained Glass
The Old School
Tempsford
Sandy
Beds
Phone: 01767 640 235
Phone: 01767 641014
Web site: www.tempsford.net
Supplies store, showroom, and studio

www.craft-fair.co.uk
Online directory of craftmakers, craft fairs, craft suppliers, and craft news

Resources *continued*

Organizations

The Glass Art Society (GAS)
1305 Fourth Avenue, Suite 711
Seattle, WA 98101, USA
Phone: (206) 382-1305
Fax: (206) 382-2630
E-mail to: info@glassart.org
Web site: www.glassart.org
The GAS is an international nonprofit organization whose purpose is to encourage excellence, to advance education, to promote the appreciation and development of the glass arts, and to support the worldwide community of artists who work with glass.
Membership is open to anyone interested in glass art.

The International Guild of Glass Artists
1025 Yorkshire Road
Grosse Pointe Park, MI 48230, USA
Phone/Fax: (313) 886-0099
E-mail: igga@warmglass.com
Web site: www.igga.org
IGGA is an international nonprofit association of artists, artisans, and craftspeople who work with glass.

Periodicals

***Glass Craftsman* magazine**
P.O. Box 678
Richboro, PA 18954, USA
Phone: (800) 786-8720; (215) 826-1799
Fax: (215) 826-1788
E-mail: custsvc@glasscraftsman.com
Web site: www.glasscraftsman.com
A bi-monthly publication that features the work of the world's top glass artists; offers tips, techniques, workshop and event information and book and video reviews.

Glass Patterns Quarterly
P.O. Box 69
Westport, KY 40077, USA
Phone: (800) 719-0769
Fax: (502) 222-4527
E-mail: gpqmag@aol.com
Web site: www.glasspatterns.com
A quarterly publication that offers instruction on glass etching, fusing, leading, copper foil, soldering, beveling, slumping, painting, overlay techniques, and more.

Gallery Artists

Arte en Vidrio (pages 98–101)

Eng. Raul Urbina Torres, Mrs. Leticia Martínez de Urbina, and Mrs. Rosario Lopéz Balam
A.P. 88 Cordemex
Mérida, Yucatán 97310, Mexico
Phone: (999) 9220081
E-mail: raulurbi@sureste.com
Web site: www.arteenvidrio.net

The artists of Arte en Vidrio create architectural glass art. They specialize in restoring the antique, European-inspired traditional glasswork in the historic homes that abound in the Yucatán region of Mexico.

Jessy Carrara (page 90)

LightGarden Glass Art Studio
1086 Washburn
Medford, OR 97501, USA
Phone: (541) 799-0272
Web site: www.lightgarden.net

Jessy Carrara creates stained, sandblasted, and fused glass art pieces. Her work includes jewelry, windows, and boxes.

Eduard Deubzer (pages 102–105)

Glashüttenweg 7
94258 Frauenau, Germany
Phone: 09926-90 20 85
Web site: www.deubzer.de

Eduard Deubzer specializes in sculptural and architectural glass art.

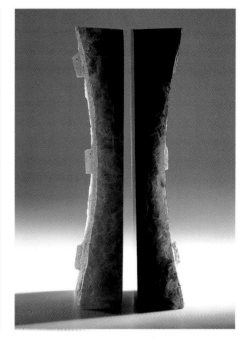

Gallery Artists *continued*

Anja Isphording (pages 106–107)

829 18th Ave. W.
Vancouver, B.C. V5Z 1W2
Canada
E-mail: anjaisphording@yahoo.de
Web site:
pages.sprint.ca/anjaisphording/files/index.htm

Anja Isphording's award-winning work is exhibited internationally from Germany to Japan. Born in Germany, she now lives and works in Canada.

Rafael Navarro Leiton (pages 96–97)

Pura Vida Glass and Clay
P.O. Box 4
Point Roberts, WA 98281, USA
Phone: (604) 278-0864
Web site: www.puravidaarts.com

Rafael Navarro Leiton has created a diverse body of work in glass and clay, including thrown ceramic pieces, and cast, slumped, fused, painted, and blown glass pieces. All of his works are original; no two are exactly alike.

Andrea and Brian Scholes (pages 91–95)

Scholes Studios
149 Mason Street
Fall River, MA 02723, USA
Phone: (508) 676-9165
Web site: www.scholesstudios.com

Andrea and Brian Scholes create custom-stained, fused, and sandblasted glass. They also make unique sand-carved stone pieces.

Acknowledgments

Livia McRee

Firstly, I'd like to thank my mother, Giorgetta … for letting me play with your expensive art markers and buying me the coveted giant box of crayons when I was little … for showing me how to use a sewing machine and how to work with glass when I grew up … and for always teaching me how to do the things I want to do, in art and life.

I would also like to thank the following people, who were all an integral part of creating this book:

Mary Ann Hall, for her support and unfailing confidence in me; Kristy Mulkern and Jennifer Hornsby, without whom nothing would ever get done; Lorraine Dey, the wonderfully talented illustrator; David Martinell; Bobbie Bush; and especially Ann Fox, for keeping it all running smoothly.

Finally, I'd like to extend a special thank you to the artists who contributed their beautiful and inspiring work for the gallery section of this book, and to Mike Sievers of Skutt Kilns for his friendly assistance.

Giorgetta McRee

I thank my daughter Livia for coming up with the idea to do this project and making that idea come true in the most creative, professional, and instructive way. She has really captured my passion for stained glass!

I also thank my son Doug and my husband Leo for being my best and worst critics, respectively, and so keeping me in check.

Mostly, I thank all the wonderful folks at Rockport Publishers who worked on this book, and through their grace and professionalism made it into a work of art.

About the Authors

Giorgetta McRee starting creating at an early age, when she learned to sew from nuns who taught her to "make the back look as good as the front." She is trained in drawing, painting, and graphic design, has taught graphic design, and sells her stained glass creations on Cape Cod in Massachusetts. She also does stained glass commissions and repair work on antique stained glass.

Livia McRee is a writer and designer. Born in Nashville and raised in New York City by her working artist parents, Livia has always been captivated by and immersed in folk and fine arts, as well as graphic design. Working on this book with her mother Giorgetta was a dream come true. She is the author of three books, *Easy Transfers for Any Surface: Crafting with Images and Photos; Quick Crafts: 30 Fast and Fun Projects;* and *Instant Fabric: Quilted Projects from Your Home Computer.*